Rucks, Pucks & Sliders

Rucks, Pucks & Sliders

More Origins of Peculiar Sporting Lingo

BOB WILSON

ICON BOOKS

Published in the UK in 2007 by
Icon Books Ltd, The Old Dairy,
Brook Road, Thriplow,
Cambridge SG8 7RG
email: info@iconbooks.co.uk
www.iconbooks.co.uk

Sold in the UK, Europe, South Africa and Asia by
Faber & Faber Ltd, 3 Queen Square,
London WC1N 3AU
or their agents

Distributed in the UK, Europe, South Africa and Asia by
TBS Ltd, TBS Distribution Centre, Colchester Road,
Frating Green, Colchester CO7 7DW

Published in Australia in 2007 by
Allen & Unwin Pty Ltd,
PO Box 8500, 83 Alexander Street,
Crows Nest, NSW 2065

Distributed in Canada by
Penguin Books Canada,
90 Eglinton Avenue East, Suite 700,
Toronto, Ontario M4P 2YE

ISBN-10: 1-84046-825-4
ISBN-13: 978-1840468-25-0

About the author

Born in Chesterfield, Bob Wilson found success playing in goal at school and gained England schoolboy honours in 1957. After qualifying as a physical education teacher at Loughborough College, he signed for Arsenal in 1963. He made more than 300 first-team appearances, helping the Gunners win the European Fairs Cup in 1970 and, one year later, the coveted League Championship and FA Cup 'double'. He also became the first English-born player to be capped for Scotland.

In 1974, he embarked on a second career in sports journalism for BBC Television. He presented *Football Focus* for twenty years and was also a regular presenter of *Match of the Day*, *Grandstand*, *Sportsnight* and *Breakfast Sport*. In August 1994, he was lured to the rival channel to be ITV's main football presenter.

An FA Full Badge Coach since 1967, he specialised in the coaching of goalkeepers for 28 years. During that time, the goalkeepers at Arsenal, Queens Park Rangers, Southampton, Tottenham and Luton benefited from his training methods. He ran his own Goalkeeping School for youngsters from 1982 until 1995. He coached the keepers at Arsenal including Pat Jennings and David Seaman.

He was Chairman of the London Football Coaches Association between 1988 and 2007. In 1989, he was awarded an honorary degree by Loughborough University for services to football. In 1997 he was appointed to the Board of Governors of the University of Hertfordshire. More recently, he was awarded honorary doctorates by the University of Derby in 2000 and Middlesex University in 2004.

He has written many books on football, mainly involving goalkeeping. These include his history of goalkeeping, *You've Got To Be Crazy* (1989), and his autobiography, *Behind the Network* (2003).

In August 1999, he and his wife Megs launched the Willow Foundation (see page 1), a charity in memory of their daughter Anna who died in December 1998. Bob and Megs have two sons: John, a radio journalist, and Robert, a photographer.

CONTENTS

The Willow Foundation

Royalties from the sale of this book will go to the Willow Foundation.

This Foundation is a national charity dedicated to providing quality of life and quality of time for seriously ill young adults (aged 16–40) through the provision of special days. The Foundation defines seriously ill as any condition that is life-threatening. To date, special days have been organised for young adults living with, among other conditions: cancer, motor neurone disease, cystic fibrosis, heart disease, organ failure and muscular dystrophy. The aim of any special day is to offer time out from treatment and allow seriously ill young adults to spend quality time with friends and/or family while pursuing an activity they all enjoy. Each special day is entirely of the applicant's choosing and is organised in meticulous detail. The Foundation funds every aspect of the chosen special day. For some, a special day is their last chance to fulfil a dream. For others, it is the opportunity to return some normality back into their lives. But for all, a special day creates precious memories for the future. Established by former Arsenal and Scotland goalkeeper and TV presenter, Bob Wilson, and his wife Megs, the Willow Foundation is a lasting memorial to their daughter, Anna, who died of cancer aged 31.

To find out more about the charity please go to: www.willowfoundation.org.uk

Introduction

I hope the fact that you're reading this book means that you enjoyed its forerunner, *Googlies, Nutmegs and Bogeys*. As sport has been played in some form or other since pretty much the beginning of civilised man, along the way it's produced a phenomenal wealth of peculiar sporting terms. It's been an absolute joy delving further into the vast library of fact and fiction of the sporting world to compile another collection of the funny, the obscure and the downright bizarre terms from a world that I've loved since I was a football-crazy kid, through my days as a physical education teacher to the Arsenal goalkeeper and finally as the TV sports presenter that I eventually became.

I very much hope you enjoy *Rucks, Pucks and Sliders* but above all, I must thank you. By purchasing a copy, you have helped put smiles on the faces of seriously ill young adults and their loved ones, at a time when they are finding it difficult to smile, through the provision of special days organised with dedication and care by the Willow Foundation, the only UK charity dedicated to the age group of 16- to 40-year olds.

Arabs

[football] – *a nickname for the fans of Dundee United FC*

This name was coined during the severe Scottish winter of 1962–63. Having already missed several games as a result of the ice and snow at Tannadice, by January 1963, United were desperate to play their Scottish Cup tie against Albion Rovers. So much so that the club hired a road-layer's tar-burner to melt the ice on the pitch. Although successful, it also removed all the grass as well. Undeterred, the club then ordered several lorry-loads of sand which they spread around the pitch before painting some lines on top. Amazingly, the referee pronounced the pitch playable, and the game got underway. United easily won the match 3-0, prompting some observers to suggest that they had taken to the sand like *Arabs*. The fans quickly adopted the name for themselves, the next few matches seeing some of them arriving at the ground wearing cobbled-together efforts at Arabian headgear.

Arkle

[cricket] – *a nickname for former Nottinghamshire and England cricketer, Derek Randall*

It was often said that Derek Randall saved at least 20 runs an innings through his prowess in the field. His hunger for the ball also often meant he could be seen actually running in from cover by the time the bowler reached the crease. He could swoop and throw in one fluid movement – and more often than not hit the stumps. Despite his agility and quality of throw, he was so fast that he would often run batsmen out simply by outpacing them to the wicket and whipping off the bails. His lightning run-out of Rick McCosker in the Test when England clinched the Ashes at Headingley in 1977 still amazes me when I think of it. It was this speed and agility that saw him nicknamed *Arkle*, after the legendary racehorse.

Perhaps the greatest steeplechase horse that has ever lived, Arkle was bought as an untried three-year-old for 1,150 guineas by Anne, Duchess of Westminster, in 1960. She named him after the mountain by Loch Stack in Sutherland, Scotland, that she could see from her home. He was fed two bottles of Guinness with his oats every day, perhaps contributing to his winning tally of three

consecutive Cheltenham Gold Cups; the King George VI Chase; the Irish Grand National; and two Hennessy Gold Cups. Such was his class that, when running in handicaps, he was forced to give away huge amounts of weight but nearly always romped home a winner. In his 34 races under rules, he carried at least twelve stone in 23 of them but finished with a career total of 27 victories. In many races, he would be allotted two or three stone more than his rivals, even though they were top-class horses in their own right. In the 1964 Irish National, the handicappers were forced to draw up two sets of weights – one for if Arkle ran, one if he didn't. Arkle had to shoulder at least two more stone than all his rivals. He still won.

back to square one

[miscellaneous] – *to start again*

Strictly speaking, this entry isn't a peculiar sporting term; it's more of a peculiar everyday term that finds its origins in sport. Nevertheless, I like it – so here it is.

On 15 January 1927, England played Wales at Twickenham. On that day, Captain Henry Blythe Thornhill 'Teddy' Wakelam, the former Harlequins rugby player, delivered the first ever live running sports commentary on the radio. With the advent of sport on the radio, the concern at the BBC was that the listener would never know where the ball was on the field. In an attempt to solve this problem, it was decided that each week the *Radio Times* would publish a grid made up of eight numbered squares that listeners could pull out and have in front of them as they listened to the commentary. Then as Wakelam identified the players and relayed what was happening, a second voice called out the number of the square the ball was in and wireless listeners around the country could follow the action on their grid. If the ball went *back to square one*, it meant that the defending side had possession of it in the very bottom left-hand corner of the pitch. And if they wanted to get themselves into an attacking position then they had to begin all over again.

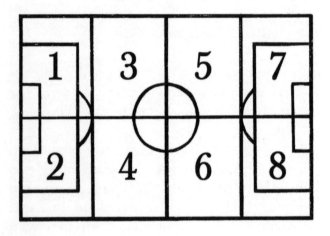

The following weekend, Captain Teddy was on duty with his microphone again, this time to watch Arsenal host Sheffield United at Highbury, and provide the first ever football commentary. To mark the 80th anniversary of that broadcast, I was recently asked to commentate on BBC Five Live for an Arsenal vs. Manchester United match for which we used the original grid commentating system. As it had died out in the 1930s, I was only mildly offended when a young producer asked me if I could remember listening to the original commentaries firsthand!

baffing spoon

[golf] – *an old equivalent to a 4-wood*

This club came from a large family of *spoons* that golfers used in the 19th century, so called because of their hollowed face. The *baffing spoon*, or *baffy* as it later became known, had a more concave face than its relatives, and was used for achieving more height over shorter distances than other spoons. It's thought that the name derives from the Old French *baffe*, meaning a blow with the back of the hand. However, the 1881 Golfer's Handbook, written by the St Andrews club manufacturer Robert Forgan, states that the baffing spoon 'is so called from the sound produced by it as it smites the ground in making the stroke'.

Baggies

[football] – *a nickname for West Bromwich Albion FC*

West Brom settled at their current home, the Hawthorns, in 1900. They soon became known as the *Throstles*, the Black Country name for the thrush, a bird seen in large numbers in the surrounding expanse of hawthorn bushes that gave their ground its name.

In its early days, the ground only had two entrances – one behind each goal. On match days, the stewards at each gate would collect the payment from fans entering the ground and place the coins in large cloth bags. When all the fans were in the ground, the stewards would then close the gates and carry the bags of money along the touchline – escorted by police – to a small office under the stand on the halfway line. Before long it became tradition for the fans to chant 'Here come the

Baggies!' as the stewards passed the main stand. Over time, the team acquired it as their nickname as well.

During my time at Arsenal, we rarely came away from the home of the Baggies with a win and the humorous taunts from their fans live on in my memory.

baggy green

[cricket] – *the famous oversized green cap worn by Australian Test cricketers*

In 1876, when Australia played their first ever Test, every player in the team was supplied with a baggy green cap as part of a parcel of equipment. This tradition continued, with not only those on debut, but the whole team being given new caps for each tour.

Over a century later in the early 1990s, an unofficial practice emerged among Australian Test cricketers to never replace their *baggy green*. Although players can obtain a replacement cap from Cricket Australia, this very rarely occurs, with the level of wear and tear becoming an unspoken symbol of seniority among the team.

In the mid-1990s, Australian Test captain Mark Taylor introduced a prematch ceremony whereby a debutant would be presented with his baggy green by the most similar player already in the team – a tradition that has since continued under the tenure of both Steve Waugh and Ricky Ponting. On one occasion, Waugh attached further symbolism to the event by having Simon Katich receive his cap from legend Richie Benaud. 'Enjoy every single moment that you wear the cap on your head' offered one of the sport's great sages, 'and respect the traditions of Australian cricket like the many that have passed before'. In order to show solidarity among the players, Taylor also made it de rigueur for the whole team to wear their baggy green for the first session in the field of each Test match. This tradition is still strictly adhered to by everyone, Shane Warne always having to wait for the second session before he could don his trademark wide-brimmed hat.

The significance of the baggy green has been reiterated by the vast sums of money they can now change hands for, with many, even of lesser-known players, fetching anything upwards of AU$10,000 (around £4,220). In 2003, the 1953 cap of Keith Miller sold at auction for AU$35,000, with Don Bradman's 1946–47 cap selling for AU$90,000 and his 1948 cap, a phenomenal AU$425,000.

bandy

[bandy] – *a sport played on ice with sticks, a ball and two teams of eleven players*

Bandy is sometimes referred to as *winter football*. Although an ancestor of ice hockey, it's contested on a rink the same size as a football pitch and by two teams of eleven players. Many of its rules, such as offside, are also the same as or very similar to those in football. Several English football clubs including Nottingham Forest and Sheffield United even had bandy in their original names. This is because when pitches froze over during the colder winters of the past, football teams used to keep themselves amused and fit by playing bandy instead.

It's thought that the sport takes its name from the verb *to bandy* meaning to toss hostile words back and forth.

Battle of Berne

[football] – *the 1954 World Cup quarter-final between Hungary and Brazil*

On 27 June 1954, Hungary met Brazil for the World Cup quarter final at the Wankdorf Stadium in the Swiss capital, *Berne*. Pitting the beautiful flamboyance of Brazil against the free-flowing football of the **Magical Magyars** should have produced a classic. Instead it produced 42 free kicks, two penalties, several mass brawls and enough cards to ultimately see three players sent off, two of whom had to be escorted from the pitch by police.

In spite of the chaos, it's widely regarded that only the magisterial refereeing of the charming Englishman Arthur Ellis prevented the game from having to be abandoned. This view wasn't shared by the Brazilian FA however, who later lodged a formal complaint to FIFA that Ellis was part of a Communist plot devised to ensure Hungary won.

At the end of the game, which Hungary eventually won 4-2, the incensed Brazilians turned off the lights in the players' tunnel and waited for the victorious Hungarians to return from the pitch. Upon their arrival, another brawl got under way in which fists, bottles and boots flew in the darkness. As the dust settled, among a list of other injuries, it became apparent that Hungarian coach Gustáv Sebes needed stitches after being struck by a broken bottle in his face. 'This was a battle; a brutal, savage match', Sebes later said. He was right, the World Cup had never seen anything like it and the British press immediately dubbed it the *Battle of Berne*.

Becher's Brook

[horse racing] – *a fence at Aintree Racecourse, near Liverpool, Merseyside*

Probably the most famous fence in sport and one I used to stand beside when previewing the Grand National for the BBC. Although only a modest 4'10" high on the side of take-off, the problems lie with a further two-foot drop on the other side. The drop used to be much more severe on the inside of the track but was levelled off in 1990 following the deaths of Brown Trix and Seeandem in the 1989 Grand National.

The fence takes its name from one Captain Martin Becher. Riding in the first ever National in 1839, his mount Conrad ploughed into the fence depositing the Captain in the brook on the other side. For the sake of his safety he had to remain in the water while the rest of the field thundered overhead. Upon emerging from the brook he is reputed to have said to a steward that he had not known 'how dreadful water tastes without the benefit of whisky'. He decided never to compete in the National again.

Bismarck

[horse racing] – *a favourite that bookmakers do not expect to win*

This term derives from the famous Second World War German battleship, named after the 19th-century German chancellor Otto von Bismarck. After it sunk the flagship and pride of the British Royal Navy, HMS *Hood*, in the Battle of the Denmark Strait on 24 May 1941, Churchill despatched every available ship with the sole intention of sinking the Bismarck.

The Bismarck was a feat of engineering for the time, with armour nearly fourteen inches thick and carrying guns with a range of 24 miles. In spite of her brawn, she was also capable of a top speed of 30 knots, making her one of the fastest ships in the world.

However, on 26 May a squadron of Swordfish torpedo bombers from the aircraft carrier Ark Royal launched an attack and hit her three times. Two of the bombs had little effect but one hit Bismarck from the rear and jammed her rudder and stearing gear, rendering her pretty much a sitting duck. Overnight, four Royal Navy boats rounded on her and the following morning, just before 9 am, started an attack that lasted nearly two hours.

Despite this pummelling, she wouldn't sink. Two Navy battleships even ran out of shells and set off for home. It wasn't until HMS *Dorsetshire* launched three final torpedoes from relatively short range that she succumbed and disappeared to the bottom of the sea. However, some strongly maintain that although the battleship's upper works were almost completely destroyed, her hull was still relatively intact – and that her own crew, rather than risk her being captured, scuttled her themselves. If this was the case it's not clear who gave the order as the ship's captain was presumed dead earlier after a sixteen-inch shell hit the bridge. Some survivors however, also report that they saw him going down alive with his ship. Either way, Bismarck, considered unsinkable by many, had lost and was on its way to the sea floor.

bolo punch

[boxing] – *a combination of a hook and an uppercut*

The key to this unconventional punch is the exaggerated and undisguised wind-up before its delivery. By making it appear obvious where the next punch is coming from, the intention is to create an element of doubt in the opponent. They're left debating whether it's a trick and if they should expect a sneaky punch from the other hand, or whether it really is a build-up to what can often be a knockout blow.

The 1930s Filipino boxer Ceferino Garcia is commonly referred to as the inventor of the punch. When asked once how he came to develop the unusual uppercut, he said that it was the same technique he used to wield a *bolo* knife while cutting sugarcane in his home country as a child. The

GARCIA

boxing media subsequently labelled it the *bolo punch* – a term that was to stick in the 1940s, when the technique was popularised by the Cuban boxer, Kid Gavilan.

However, it appears that the first practitioner of the punch was another Filipino boxer by the name of Macario Flores.

According to a copy of Washington's *Tacoma News Tribune* from 27 March 1924: 'Flores lets his right hand go just as his countrymen throw a bolo knife. The blow is not only hard, but it is as fast as a streak of lightning, being almost impossible to follow with the human eye.'

Booming Cannon

[football] – *a nickname for Hungarian legend Ferenc Puskás*

He was short, stocky, barrel-chested, overweight, couldn't head the ball and pretty much only used his left foot. Nevertheless, his left foot is perhaps the greatest the football world has ever seen and he is, without question, one of my favourite players of all time.

Born in Budapest on 2 April 1927, Ferenc Puskás began his career as a junior with Kispest Athletic Club where he played under an assumed identity – Miklós Kovács – until his twelfth birthday, when he was officially old enough to join in. He made his professional

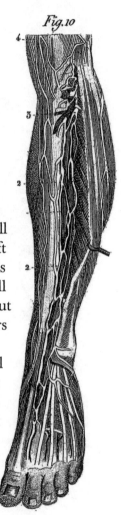

Fig.10

debut at the club aged sixteen. In 1949, as Communist rule spread across Eastern Europe, Kipest was taken over by the Hungarian Army and its name changed to Honvéd. As a military institution, players were assigned ranks and, in time, Puskás was appointed a major. He went on to win five Hungarian League titles with the club, scoring 357 goals in 349 games. He became known as the *Galloping Major*.

In 1956, while Honvéd was on tour in Spain, the Hungarian Revolution erupted in Budapest. When the uprising was crushed by the invading Soviet Union, many of the team, including Puskás, decided not to return. It effectively saw the break up of not only Honvéd, but the great Hungarian national side, the **Magical Magyars**. This team had dominated world football throughout the 1950s, with the Galloping Major scoring 84 goals in 85 international appearances since his debut, aged eighteen.

Puskás was suspended from football for two years by FIFA at the behest of the Hungarian FA which branded him a traitor. In 1958, at the age of 31 and considerably overweight, he was signed by Real Madrid. In the next nine years, he played 261 matches for the Spanish giants, scoring 236 times. He was *pichichi* on four occasions, guiding the club to five consecutive La Liga titles and three European Cups. To Real fans – as an extension of his existing military nickname and because he possessed the most searing left foot they had ever seen – he became known as the *Booming Cannon*.

As far back as 1953, I remember watching him play at Wembley against England. I was utterly transfixed as he controlled the ball with his left foot, dragged it back and sent England captain Billy Wright the wrong way, 'like a fireman running to the wrong fire' as one paper said – before lashing an unstoppable shot past England keeper Gilbert Merrick. It was one of the best individual goals I have ever seen.

boxing

[boxing] – *a combat sport in which two competitors trade punches with fists enclosed in leather gloves*

Although fighting with fists as a sport can be traced back to earlier than 4,000 BC, the term *boxing* did not come into use for another six millennia. Having almost entirely died out as a sport right across Europe with the fall of the Roman Empire in AD 476, it was not until 1681 that the *London Protestant Mercury* documented England's first bare-knuckle *prizefight*. In 1719, James Figg became the first heavyweight boxing champion. With the introduction of the title, came the sport's name: it was considered that the clenching of the fist with the thumb laid over the fingernails – as was the style at that time – formed a so-called *box*, and so the throwing of these fists came to be known as boxing.

Brickyard

[motor racing] – *a nickname for the Indianapolis Motor Speedway, Indiana, USA*

Home of the legendary Indianapolis 500, host of the US Grand Prix*, and self-proclaimed Racing Capital of the World, the Speedway's glorious history had an inauspicious start. When it opened in August 1909, the track was made simply of coarse crushed rock and tar – a surface that was to prove disastrous. Its very first race was stopped less then halfway through and, after a continued spate of horrific accidents, the track was abandoned after only a few days' use.

In the autumn of that year a new surface was built: 3.2 million paving bricks were imported by rail from the Western part of the state, laid on their sides in a bed of sand and secured with mortar. Indianapolis Motor Speedway had become the *Brickyard*.

* For more on *Grand Prix* see Appendix, page 182.

In 1936, asphalt began to be applied to the rougher parts of the circuit, and by 1939 only 650 yards of bricks on the main straight remained. This section survived until 1961 when it too was covered over, except for three feet of bricks at the start and finish line. This symbolic strip and the Speedway's nickname have both remained as a nostalgic reminder of its glorious and chequered past.

bullseye

[darts] – *the central spot of the dartboard, worth 50 points*

The term *bullseye* was first used towards the end of the 16th century as a name for the thick spherical piece of glass that was set into the deck of a wooden ship to help illuminate the gun decks below. The name gained popular usage over the following century to describe pretty much anything that was small, round or spherical. By the 18th century, with the proper advent of archery as a sport rather than simply an instrument of war, a standard target was used for which the central spot also became known as the bullseye. In time, the term was adopted by the game of darts with the development of its board and the similar, albeit smaller, central spot.

The increasing number of modern dartboards with black rather than the traditionally red bullseyes has seen the advent of the term *striking oil* for those that manage to hit it.

can of corn

[baseball] – *an easy catch for a fielder*

It's thought that this term originated towards the end of the 19th century, deriving from the traditional habit of American groceries at that time to stack canned goods high against the wall behind the counter. A sales clerk would then use a wooden stick to knock the cans individually from the top of the display when needed, before catching them easily with an open hand or outstretched apron.

Canaries

[football] – *the nickname for Norwich City FC*

Norwich City FC was formed by a group of friends in 1902. Their song, 'On the ball, City', is thought to be the world's oldest football song still in use today. Originally the team was nicknamed the *Citizens* and played in blue and white halved shirts with white shorts.

Canary-breeding was a pastime practised by a large number of people in Norfolk at that time, including one of the early managers at the club who often referred to his players as his *Canaries*. By the summer of 1907, the name had gained sufficient popularity that the team began to wear yellow shirts.

With crowds continuing to grow and the landlords of the team's ground placing unworkable terms in a proposed new lease, a new venue was required. And so, in 1908, they moved to *Ruymp's*

Hole, a disused ancient chalk pit in Rosary Road. The stands from their previous home at Newmarket Road were ferried across the city by horse and cart and built precariously into the steep quarry sides, resulting in a football ground unlike any other. It became known as the *Nest*, and it was there that the name Canaries well and truly stuck.

catgut

[tennis] – *a strong cord used for stringing racquets*

Natural gut has been used for sports racquet strings for centuries – taken from a number of animals but never from a cat. So why is it called *catgut*, when the thought of using moggy's intestines to produce searing cross-court winners continues to horrify cat lovers across the world?

In the Middle Ages, Welsh troubadours played a type of fiddle that supposedly sounded like a cat meowing. The English, not particularly impressed with the instrument, referred to it as the *cat*, and to the strings making the peculiar noise as catgut. By the 14th century, when natural gut was also used to string the very first sports racquets, the name had already stuck.

chequered flag

[motor racing] – *a black-and-white flag waved at cars as they cross the finish line to signal the end of the race*

The true origin of the chequered flag seems to be lost in time but several theories abound. Some believe that it originated with horse racing during the early days of the settlement of the American Midwest; the racing would be followed by large public meals and to signal that the food was ready and that the racing should come to an end, the women would wave a large chequered tablecloth. Others think that it evolved from the early days of the Tour de France when stewards wore black-and-white chequered vests to indicate to cyclists which way to go. In time, the chequered material was placed on flagpoles instead, including one at the end of each stage. However, probably the most likely – but unfortunately least interesting – theory, is that it was chosen simply because it was easily seen against the multi-coloured background of spectators and buildings in early races.

choke

[golf] – *to crack under the pressure and lose from a seemingly winning position at the climax of a tournament*

Although this can of course occur in any sport, it's perhaps most easily detected within professional stroke-play golf. Arguably its most severe example came at the Masters at Augusta in 1996. In the opening round, Australian Greg Norman carded a course-record 63. Three days later he managed to go round the same eighteen holes in fifteen strokes more. His brilliance over the first three rounds had seen him start the final day with a six-stroke lead – the biggest in Masters' history – over Nick Faldo, his nearest rival. He looked set to take home his first Green Jacket*. However, by the back nine, Norman had surrendered his lead, and by the 18th green, the tearful Australian had fallen a further five shots behind the victorious Faldo, in one of the most dramatic collapses in Major Championship golf.

* For more on *Green Jacket* see Appendix, page 183.

Although only gaining widespread usage in the 1960s, the term is thought to have originated with the Salem witch trials in the 17th century. Women were made to eat a Holy Communion wafer, the rationale being that a witch would find it impossible to swallow. Although a relatively simple task, with their life at stake, a large number of women were found guilty and executed as a result of *choking* under the pressure.

Clockwork Orange

[football] – *a nickname for the Dutch national team in the 1970s*

Although the Dutch national flag of red, white and blue is the oldest tricolour still in use today, the country's national football team play in bright orange. This comes from the coat of arms of William I of Orange – or *Father of the Fatherland* as he is known in the Netherlands – the main leader of the Dutch revolt against the Spanish in the 16th century.

From nowhere, the 1970s saw the emergence of Holland as a true footballing superpower, reaching consecutive World Cup finals in 1974 and 1978. This was largely due to their perfection of *Total Football*, or *totaalvoetbal*, a system pioneered by legendary coach Rinus Michels. In this system, if a player moves out of position, their role is immediately filled by a team-mate leaving the team formation intact. Holland became so proficient in using total football that the side became known as the *Clockwork Orange*.

I had the pleasure of playing against the brilliant Johann Cruyff-inspired Orange in 1971 in my second international appearance for Scotland. We managed to hold them to 1-1 in Amsterdam's Olympic Stadium until Ajax's Barry Hulshoff scored their winner in the very last minute!

condor

[golf] – *a score of four under par* on a hole*

Otherwise known as a *double-albatross** or *triple-eagle**, this incredibly rare event takes its name from the *condor* – the largest flying landbird in the Western hemisphere. This New World species of vulture is virtually extinct, and is equally rare in the golfing world: the condor has been achieved on only three known occasions.

On 15 November 1962, at Hope Country Club in Arkansas, USA, American Larry Bruce took his drive over a cluster of pine trees on the 480-yard sharp-right dogleg par-5 5th hole. By cutting out the dogleg and clearing the trees he reached the green in one, the ball miraculously disappearing into the hole. Bruce died in 2001 but still remains a local legend.

On 24 July 1995, at Teign Valley Golf Club in Christow, England, Irishman Shaun Lynch also successfully took on a sharp dogleg 496-yard par-5 by hitting a 3-iron left off the tee over a 25-foot hedge. It went in, he went on to shoot an 88, bought drinks for all and sundry, and was subsequently given lifelong honorary membership to the club.

There's only one condor to have ever occurred on a straight par-5. On 4 July 2002, at the Green

Valley Ranch Golf Club in Denver, Colorado, American Michael J. Crean hit a driver off the tee of the 517-yard 9th hole. A combination of incline, hard ground, thin air (Denver is a mile above sea level) and tail wind of 30 miles per hour saw the ball travel the unbelievable distance and go in the hole. It's the longest hole-in-one ever recorded.

* For more on *par*, *albatross* and *eagle*, see Appendix, pages 191, 179 and 181.

Cottagers

[football] – *a nickname for Fulham FC*

In 1780, William Craven built a cottage where the centre circle of the Fulham pitch currently resides. The cottage was surrounded by woodland which made up part of Anne Boleyn's hunting grounds. It was lived in by a number of people for the next century until destroyed by fire in 1888. Following the fire, the site was abandoned.

Fifteen years later, it was discovered by representatives from Fulham FC who were looking for a site on which to establish a permanent home for the club. The land was so overgrown that it took nearly two years to make it suitable for football. The pitch saw its first match in 1896 and the team's new home was named Craven Cottage.

In 1905, the club called in Glasgow-born engineer and factory architect Archibald Leitch to construct a stadium. He built what's known today as the Johnny Haynes Stand, a listed building that remains one of the finest examples of football architecture, making the ground one of the most picturesque settings in league football today. However, Leitch forgot to accommodate some changing rooms in his final plans and so built the famous cottage that still stands in the corner of the ground today. Nevertheless it cemented the ground's name as Craven Cottage, and over time the team became known as the *Cottagers*.

My abiding memory of playing at the Cottage should be of proudly facing the likes of Johnny Haynes and England World Cup hero George Cohen. Instead, it's of dislocating my elbow in the first ten minutes of a game and managing to continue in goal for the remaining 80 minutes. We lost 1-0 to a Graham Leggat free kick.

Coupe Aéronautique Gordon Bennett

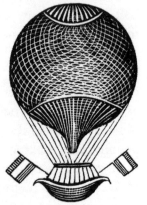

[ballooning] – *the sport's oldest and most celebrated event, the aim of which is to fly the furthest distance from the launch site*

James Gordon Bennett Jr. was publisher of the *New York Herald* in the late 19th century. He led the expensive and flamboyant lifestyle of a true playboy, indulging in yachts and lavish mansions. He was the youngest ever Commodore of the New York Yacht Club, served in the Navy during the Civil War, and in 1866, won the first transoceanic boat race.

However, he often courted controversy with his behaviour. On one occasion he arrived late and drunk to a party at the family mansion of his fiancée, socialite Caroline May, and then proceeded to urinate into the fireplace in front of his hosts and fellow guests. This would give rise to the phrase *Gordon Bennett!* as an exclamation of disbelief.

In 1906 he sponsored the *Coupe Aéronautique Gordon Bennett* which, in its inaugural race, saw sixteen balloons set off from the Tuileries Gardens in Paris, France. The winners, Americans Frank P. Lahm and his co-pilot Henry B. Hersey, landed their balloon 22 hours later in Fylingdales in North Yorkshire.

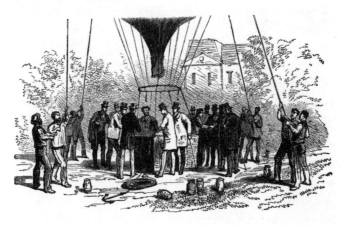

In the 1995 race, three balloons entered Belarusian air space. Despite the race organisers having informed the Belarusian government beforehand and the flight plans having been filed, the Belarusian air force shot down one of the balloons, killing the two American competitors on board. In spite of this horrendous incident, the Coupe Aéronautique Gordon Bennett still continues today.

Crazylegs

[American football] – *a nickname for the great Elroy Hirsch*

Running back and receiver Elroy Hirsch is widely regarded as one of the best American football players of all time. He spent the majority of his professional career at the Los Angeles Rams but acquired his nickname while playing in his first college season, with the Wisconsin Badgers in 1942. In a game away to the Great Lakes Naval Training Station, Hirsch ran 61 yards for a touchdown in the third quarter. The next morning while travelling back on the train, one of his team-mates was reading the match report in the *Chicago Daily News*, which recounted the touchdown. Journalist Francis Powers had written that Hirsch 'ran like a demented duck. His crazy legs were gyrating in six different directions all at the same time.'

'Hey, Ghost, this says you have crazy legs!' his team-mate exclaimed. 'Hey, Crazylegs!' and the name remained with him for the rest of his life.

Crow's Nest

[golf] – *a room in the clubhouse of the Augusta National Golf Club, where five amateurs can stay during the Masters**

Augusta's famous clubhouse was built in 1854 and is reputedly the first cement house ever constructed in America's Deep South. High up in the clubhouse, just below the building's famous eleven-foot-square windowed cupola, is the *Crow's Nest*. This is a single room divided into several partitions, three containing single beds; another with two beds; and a sitting area with a game table, sofa and chairs, television and telephone. There is also a bathroom and an additional sink.

Predominantly, it takes its name from being at the top of the clubhouse, a similar vantage point as a crow's nest at the top of a tree. In addition, some think the term *nest* evolved because it represents a small space in which the amateurs live before coming of age – emerging to play in the Masters, the first major of the golfing year.

* For more on *Masters* see Appendix, page 188.

Curse of the Bambino

[baseball] – *the reason cited for the failure of the Boston Red Sox to win the World Series in the 84-year period from 1920 until 2004*

In 1914, a teacher at St Mary's School in Baltimore, USA, brought George Herman Ruth Jr. to the attention of Jack Dunn, the owner of the Orioles baseball team. Upon seeing Ruth pitch, Dunn immediately signed him up to the team. Some of the older players in the side began referring to him as 'Jack's newest babe'. Babe Ruth moved to the Boston Red Sox later that year and in time would also become known as the *Bambino*, the Italian for *babe*.

Six years at the Red Sox saw Ruth become their star player, helping them to World Series titles in 1915, 1916 and 1918. A couple of years later, Red Sox owner Harry Frazee decided to sell the Bambino to the New York Yankees (who had never won a championship) to raise money for the production of his girlfriend's musical *No, No, Nanette*. Over the next 84 years, the Yankees won 26 World Series titles while the Red Sox won none, often losing to the Yankees in the most peculiar and heart-breaking circumstances. As the years passed, people began to ascribe Boston's continuing failure to the *Curse of the Bambino*.

The curse was finally lifted in 2004 when the Red Sox won the World Series (weirdly with a total lunar eclipse presiding over the ballpark – the first during any World Series game) after making an unprecedented comeback to defeat the Yankees in the American League Championship. The following year, the contract that saw the Bambino move from Boston to New York, sold at Sotheby's for US$996,000.

Curse of the Rainbow Jersey

[cycling] – *a term used to describe the terrible luck bestowed upon those that wear the distinctive jersey of the reigning world champion in a particular racing event*

In 1965, Britain's Tommy Simpson won the world title and the prospect of a lucrative following season wearing the rainbow jersey lay ahead. That winter he broke his leg while skiing.

In 1970 Belgian Jean-Pierre Monseré became the youngest cycling World Champion of all time. He was killed the following year when hit by a car during a race.

On 24 September 2006, Italian Paolo Bettini was crowned World Champion. Eight days later, his brother, who was organising a celebration of the capture of the rainbow jersey, died in a car crash, metres from his home.

In November 2006, while wearing the rainbow jersey of World Madison Champion, Spain's Isaac Gálvez collided with another competitor during a race and subsequently hit a railing. He died on the way to hospital.

These incidents and the numerous others have ensured that even some of the most cynical have begun to believe in the *Curse of the Rainbow Jersey*.

Devil's Own

[darts] – *a score of 88*

This term takes its name from the 88th division of the Connaught Rangers, a regiment of the British Army raised in 1793 from the men of Connaught in Ireland by John Thomas de Burgh, 13th Earl of Clanricard. After distinguished service in the Peninsular, Crimean, Boer and First World Wars, the regiment was disbanded in 1922 following the foundation of the Irish Free State.

During the Peninsular War at the beginning of the 19th century, the 88th had served under Lieutenant-General Sir Thomas Picton, who ultimately became the most senior officer to die at Waterloo. Picton had been scathing of them at first, referring to them as the *Connaught Footpads* in reference to their reputation for plundering. It wasn't long, however, before he learned to appreciate their abilities when it came to a hard fight. There's much evidence to suggest that in moments of crisis in battle on the Iberian Peninsula, Picton would specifically send in the 88th to try and secure that part of the frontline. Their repeated success and the manner in which it was achieved saw Picton name them the *Devil's Own*.

Doggett's Coat and Badge

[rowing] – *the prize and name of the oldest rowing race in the world*

At the beginning of the 18th century there were more than 10,000 watermen licensed to work on the Thames above London Bridge, ferrying passengers along and across the river before the grand era of bridge-building had begun. Thomas Doggett, an Irish actor plying his trade in London at the time, became very dependent on watermen to ferry him back and forth between his places of work and his residence in Chelsea. In 1715, Doggett fell overboard while crossing the Thames near Embankment but was rescued by a waterman. In appreciation, he organised and funded a race from the Swan pub at London Bridge to the Swan pub at Chelsea to be contested by six apprentice watermen. In honour of King George I, the inaugural race took place on 1 August 1715 to commemorate the first anniversary of his accession to the throne. Doggett provided the prize of a resplendent red coat and silver badge.

The four-mile, five-furlong* race continued to be organised and funded by Doggett each year until his death in 1721. In his will, he left specific instructions and bequeathed money to the Worshipful Company of Fishmongers to ensure the continuation of the race. It has faithfully complied with his wishes ever since, making this the world's oldest-known sporting contest still in existence.

* For more on *furlong* see Appendix, page 182.

The Don

[cricket] – *a nickname for Australian legend, Donald Bradman*

Sir Donald George Bradman AC is, beyond any argument, the greatest batsman who ever lived. At the age of nineteen, he made his first-class debut and scored 118. At 21, he made 452 not out for New South Wales against Queensland at Sydney, the highest score ever made in first-class cricket across the world at that time. In the same year, he scored 974 runs in only seven innings over the course of the five Ashes Tests, the highest individual total in any Test series the world has ever seen. On one day of that series he scored 309, still the most runs scored by an individual in a single day's play. Against South Africa the following year, he recorded the highest batting average for a five-Test series there has ever been, with 201.50.

Bradman scored centuries at a rate better than one every three innings. He converted very nearly a third of them into double hundreds, his career total of 37 first-class double centuries still the most achieved by any batsman in the history of the game.

One phase of his career saw him score centuries in eight consecutive Tests, amassing the following scores: 270, 212, 169, 144 not out, 102 not out, 103, 187 and 234. His 270, in the third Test against England at the Melbourne Cricket Ground in 1937, is still rated by *Wisden* as the greatest Test innings of all time.

His career Test batting average of 99.94 is considered by some to be the greatest statistical performance in any major sport. The Australian Broadcasting Corporation obviously thought so, as they have since made their mailing address of every state capital, PO Box 9994, in honour of his remarkable achievement.

There are too many more records to mention. As former Australian batsman Jack Fingleton once remarked: 'You didn't bat with Bradman, you ran for him.'

The sport might well never see a player of his stature again. And that is why he became *The Don*.

Duel in the Sun

[golf] – *the 18th hole on Turnberry's Ailsa course*

In 1977, Turnberry hosted the Open for the first time. It turned out to be a classic showdown between two of the game's giants. In blistering summer heat, Jack Nicklaus and Tom Watson matched each other in every round until the last, when Nicklaus shot a 66 to Watson's 65, finishing the Championship ten and eleven shots clear of the field respectively, with their 268 and 269 destroying the tournament record of 276. In recognition of this classic battle, the 18th has since been named the *Duel in the Sun*.

early bath

[rugby league] – *a red card*

Although now used by other commentators in other sports, this phrase was coined by the ebullient Yorkshireman Eddie Waring, while commentating a rugby league match in the 1960s. Played predominantly in the North of England and often in its characteristic wet weather, rugby league encounters sometimes descend into a total mud-bath, with players becoming so covered in mud that it's impossible to identify them. With no players' names at his disposal, Waring would then spruce up the other aspects of his commentary to keep the viewers entertained. In one match, with the camera focusing on an indeterminate spherical object he was forced to admit: 'I don't know if that is his head or the ball. We'll see if it stands up.' Another afternoon saw the birth of the term *up-and-under* for a high kick, and when a player was sent off late in the game, Waring declared that he had been packed-off for an *early bath.*

Eddie was a lovely sensitive man and this side of his nature came out with his reaction at the climax of the memorable Challenge Cup in 1968. Wakefield Trinity scored a try in the last minute to narrow the score to 11-10, leaving Don Fox with the seemingly simple task of kicking a conversion from in front of the posts to secure victory. However, he slipped on the saturated pitch and missed, handing the victory to Leeds. As Fox slumped in the Wembley mud, Eddie's commentary was simple and perfect: 'Eee, poor lad.'

Eddie would go

[surfing] – *a reference to legendary waterman Eddie Aikau, renowned for taking on waves from which others would shy away*

In 1968, 21-year-old Hawaiian surfing legend Eddie Aikau became the first lifeguard hired by the City and County of Honolulu to work on the North Shore, and given the impossible task of covering miles of coastline. He saved dozens of lives over the next three years, perhaps hundreds, as he hardly ever filed official rescue reports. In 1971, the roving patrol was disbanded and he was assigned permanently to the infamous Waimea Bay. Not a single life was ever lost on his watch.

On 16 March 1978, Aikau, keen to honour his Hawaiian heritage, set sail as part of a crew on 2,500-mile journey that would follow the ancient route of migration between Hawaii and Tahiti. During the journey, their voyaging canoe, Hokule'a, developed a leak in one of its two hulls and later capsized in extremely stormy weather. They spent a night clinging to the overturned hull. In spite of being battered by waves and gale-force winds and not knowing how far they were from land, Aikau insisted on going for help. He tied the surfboard leash to his ankle, a portable strobe light and some oranges around his neck, and hesitantly tied a life jacket around his waist. As he  paddled away, crew members held hands and said a prayer. Some saw Aikau ditch the cumbersome life jacket a few hundred yards from the Hokule'a. They all watched as he and his board peeked back and forth into view as it rode up and over the huge waves. He gradually became smaller and smaller as he stroked away until eventually he vanished from sight.

Although the Hokule'a was spotted by a plane later that day and its crew saved, no-one ever saw Eddie Aikau again. Nevertheless, his name would be immortalised by the term that emerged and gained widespread usage with watermen across the world after his death – *Eddie would go.*

Eel

[swimming] – *the nickname for Eric Moussambani*

Equatorial Guinea's Eric Moussambani was invited to compete in the 100-metre freestyle at the 2000 Sydney Olympics through a programme that allows a handful of athletes to compete even though they don't meet qualifying standards – an initiative introduced to spread sport around the world. He had taken up swimming only eight months before the Olympics, and until reaching Sydney had never seen a 50-metre pool.

In the heats he squared off against two other swimmers, but they were both disqualified for false starts. Moussambani was left to swim the heat by himself and having never swum that far before, only just managed to get to the finishing line to secure his place in the final. Craig Lord, the swimming correspondent for *The Times*, immediately wrote an article about 'Equatorial Guinea's aquatic answer to Eddie the Eagle – Eric the *Eel*'. Before long, the name had stuck.

In the final, while the eventual winner Pieter van den Hoogenband managed a world-record-breaking 47.84 seconds, Moussambani took more than twice as long. He splashed his way to the finish line to the rapturous applause of the 20,000-strong Sydney crowd, outside even the 200-metre world record time. 'The last fifteen metres were very difficult', Moussambani said.

Everest of the sea

[sailing] – *a nickname for the Vendée Globe*

The Vendée Globe is a solo, non-stop round-the-world race in which assistance is absolutely forbidden. The inaugural race was in 1989–90 and it's since been held every four years. It is the only race of its kind in the world.

Entrants set off from France in November, sail down the Atlantic Ocean to the Cape of Good Hope on the coast of South Africa, then clockwise around Antarctica. Keeping Cape Leeuwin (on the south-west coast of Australia) and

Cape Horn (on the south coast of Chile) to port, competitors proceed back up to France, aiming to complete the course by February.

A significant proportion of the entrants retire each year, usually as a result of the severe conditions they encounter in the South Pacific. In 1992, in only the second edition of the race and only four days after the start, British sailor Nigel Burgess was found drowned off Cape Finisterre on the west coast of Spain. It's thought that he fell overboard.

Four years later, on 8 January 1997, Canadian Gerry Roufs was in second place when his satellite positioning beacon stopped transmitting. Despite four competitors combing the ocean he couldn't be found. Later that year on 16 July, long after the race had finished, a Panamanian cargo ship found the battered remains of Roufs's boat drifting 300 miles off the coast of Chile.

Like those that have died trying to reach the summit of the highest mountain on Earth over the years, these two men lost their lives attempting to conquer the *Everest of the sea*, the highest pinnacle in the yachting world.

falling leaf

[football] – *a long-range shot which sees the ball change direction radically in the course of its flight*

In my playing era, footballs were made of thick heavy leather, which got even heavier when it rained. They went from a to b in a straight line and that was it. At the 1970 World Cup, a combination of Mexico's thin air and the unique ability of Brazil's legendary **Garrincha** to hit across the ball produced the first dramatic swerve I had ever seen. However, these days, the modern football is much lighter and if hit hard enough moves around in the air erratically enough to give the keeper a real headache. One swerve and it's a *banana*, two and it's a *falling leaf*, mimicking the path of a leaf buffeted by the air. Probably the most famous example of this came at the Tournoi de France in 1997, when another Brazilian, Roberto Carlos, blasted a 37-yard free kick wide of the French wall. Although it seemed to be easily heading out for a goal kick, it took a devastating left swerve at the last minute and ricocheted off the inside of the post into the net. The French goalkeeper at the time, Fabien Barthez, hadn't even moved.

fevvers

[darts] – *a score of 33*

This derives from the 19th-century cockney tongue-twister:'Thirty-three thousand feathers on a thrush's throat'. In the early 20th century, London's East End was home to the dartboard manufacturing industry. As result, a large number of public houses and working men's clubs in the area had a board. The game was rife among East Enders and much of its terminology was invented at that time. So although 33 was initially represented by the term *feathers*, in a nod to their dialect, it has been assumed that a proper cockney would have said: 'Firty-free fahsand *fevvers* on a frush's froat.'

Fiery

[cricket] – *a nickname for Yorkshire and England fast bowler, Fred Trueman*

Frederick Sewards Trueman was larger than life from the word go. Born in Stainton near Maltby, West Riding (now South Yorkshire) on 6 February 1931, he weighed in at a whopping 14 pounds 1 ounce. In 1949 he made his first-class debut for Yorkshire at the tender age of seventeen. Only four years later he made his Test debut after being granted leave from his National Service in the Royal Air Force. With his trademark scowl and mop of unruly jet-black hair, Trueman inspired a seven-wicket victory for England after India were reduced to 0-4 at the start of their second innings, with three of the batsman dismissed by the Yorkshireman in the space of eight deliveries. In his third Test he took 8 for 31 – the best Test bowling figures by a genuinely fast bowler at the time. He became a schoolboy hero of mine as the first man in the history of the game to take 300 Test wickets. Over time, Trueman's extreme pace, ability to intimidate batsmen psychologically, and his generally aggressive approach to the game, saw him labelled simply *Fiery*, or *Fiery Fred.*

John Arlott said of him: 'The kindling could be sudden and unexpected. All that anyone knew was that suddenly he was going eagerly back to his mark; there was a belligerent spring in his run, he came over like a storm-wave breaking on a beach, and followed through with so mighty a heave that the knuckles of his right hand swept the ground ... Where previously the ball had curved off the pitch calf-high, it now spat to the hips or ribs: wicket-keeper and slips moved deeper; the batsman, who had seemed established, was late on his stroke; and the whole match was transformed.'

Off the pitch, one of his favourite tricks was to go into the opposition dressing room prior to a match and say: 'Right, there's five wickets in here for me to start with.' In an Ashes Test in the early 1960s, as an Australian batsman emerged from the pavilion and turned to shut the boundary gate, Trueman suggested: 'Don't bother son. You'll be back soon enough.' His ability to out-psyche batsmen only served to add to his considerable physical capabilities. In his prime there were only a handful of batsman that could play Trueman with any real certainty and as a result captains would throw him the ball at every conceivable opportunity. This ensured he bowled more than 99,000 deliveries in first-class cricket. He still holds the record for the most consecutive first-class matches played in which he took a wicket (67). In spite of his massive workload he hardly missed a game through injury, his only admission of fatigue coming after he had taken his world record 300th Test wicket at the Oval in 1964. Asked whether he thought his achievement would ever be surpassed, he remarked: 'I don't know, but whoever does it will be bloody tired.'

I met Fred on a couple of occasions towards the end of his life. Both times he was friendly but characteristically blunt and I still smile when I think of our first meeting: 'Aye lad, tha's done well for thee self, except for that bad goal you let in at Cup Final!'

Upon his death on 1 July 2006, Sir John Major paid fitting tribute to the great man: 'Fred Trueman was one of the great fast bowlers of all time. He became an icon in his pomp, and remained so all his life. England has lost a national treasure and history has gained a legend.'

fish and globe

[darts] – *a score of 45*

Until the second half of the 20th century this was more commonly known as a *bag o' nuts*. The reason being, when competing on a fairground darts stall, a score of 45 would traditionally win the customer a small paper bag of peanuts. Over the following decades, however, it became more likely that a customer would be offered a goldfish in a jar or *globe*, which, in time, saw the term updated. Although some think that the term globe was chosen as a result of stall owners talking up the jar in the prize, it may be because the traditional shakeable snowglobes were becoming popular at that time and might also have been offered as a prize. Either way, if you score 45, then you've bagged yourself a *fish and globe*.

flat-track bully

[cricket] – *a specialist batsman who is only very good when batting on a benign pitch*

This term was coined by New Zealand cricketer John Bracewell back in 1989. He was referring to Graham Hick who was spending the winters of 1987–88 and 1988–89 playing in New Zealand's domestic competition for Northern Districts. Hick was enjoying great success, notching up ten centuries and averaging 63.61 in the first season and 94.46 in the second. In one game against Auckland he scored a first-class record of 173 runs between tea and the close of play!

This moniker dogged Hick throughout his career, and Bracewell's accusation would come back to haunt him in equal measure fifteen years later. Now New Zealand coach, Bracewell took his touring side to Worcestershire at the start of their summer tour. With preparations for the summer ahead very much in mind, Bracewell looked on in desperation as a 37-year-old Hick dismantled his bowling strikeforce, despatching them around the picturesque Worcester ground on his way to an unbeaten 204. As Derek Pringle succinctly put it: 'Hick made a run-a-ball double hundred against the cream of the crop on a pitch never as easy as his strokes made it appear.' You could say it was retribution complete.

Foinavon

[horse racing] – *a fence at Aintree Racecourse, near Liverpool, Merseyside*

A fence only 4'6" high shouldn't pose too much of a problem. Nevertheless in the 1967 Grand National it caused carnage on an unprecedented scale. On the second circuit of the world-famous steeplechase*, there were a few riderless horses at the front of the leading pack. When they reached the fence, the loose horses had decided they weren't going over and bolted across the track. This frightened the leaders still carrying jockeys* who pulled up and refused to jump the fence. Before long there was a total pile-up with a number of jockeys being flung over the fence while their horses remained on the other side. As horses stopped ploughing into the melee and the chaos gradually untangled, none of the horses had any speed with which to jump the fence and so were forced to run the wrong way down the track so that they could come back and give it a second try.

In the meantime, a 100/1 rank outsider by the name of

Foinavon who was so far behind that he had missed the bedlam, caught up and quietly picked his way through the aftermath. He was the only horse to jump the fence at the first attempt that day and made it across with a 100-yard lead. Seventeen horses had remounted and were now in hot pursuit. Although there still a further seven fences to go, Foinavon just managed to hold on – and today, his name remains with the fence that allowed him to become the most unlikely winner the Grand National has ever seen.

* For more on *steeplechase* and *jockey* see Appendix, pages 192 and 185.

football

[football] – *a sport played with a round inflated ball on a playing field with two goals by two teams of eleven players*

Man has been kicking a ball around for at least two millennia. Nevertheless, before the formation of the FA in 1863 and the subsequent introduction of a set of rules, *football* was a rowdy affair with opposing factions fighting pitched battles with the 'goals' sometimes several miles apart. Although the use of foot was the main way of propelling the ball in the mass throng of writhing bodies, the name referred to the fact that it was a game of *ball*, or *gameball*, played on foot. This helped distinguish it from the team games of the disapproving nobility, which were played on horseback.

Irrespective of the disapproving nobility of the past, I owe an awful lot to the game and one of my favourite quotes comes from the philosopher and fellow goalkeeper Albert Camus who once said: 'All that I know most surely about morality and the obligations of man I owe to football.'

futsal

[futsal] – *a form of **football** played indoors with a less bouncy ball and five players on each side*

Futsal was devised by Juan Carlos Ceriani in Montevideo, Uraguay, in 1930 – the same year that the country hosted the first FIFA World Cup. It soon spread to South America, particularly Brazil, where  many of the country's great footballers including Pelé, Zico, Sócrates and Ronaldinho have cut their teeth on the futsal pitch. Its name is an amalgam of the Spanish *fútbol* (football) and *sala* (room), which can be very roughly translated as indoor football.

Galáctico

[football] – *a world-famous and highly paid attacking player signed by Spanish La Liga club, Real Madrid*

During Real Madrid's rich and chequered history, the club and its players have acquired a number of nicknames. Among the earliest were *Los Blancos* and *Los Merengues* with reference to the team's famous all-white strip. In the 1970s, the signing of several northern European players saw them labelled *Los Vikingos*.

In 2000, despite the club having just won its second European Cup in three years, Lorenzo Sanz lost the club presidency to former politician Florentino Pérez. Instrumental in his success was his promise to lure Portugese star Luís Figo to the Bernabéu from FC Barcelona should he be elected. On 16 July, Pérez won the coveted job. Eight days later, Luís Figo was presented with the number 10 shirt of Real Madrid. It marked the start of Pérez's policy to bring one of the best footballers in the world to the club each summer whatever the cost. At £38.7 million, the signing of Figo set a world record transfer fee. The following summer, Pérez signed Frenchman Zinedine Zidane from Juventus for £44 million – another world record.

Before long, each high-profile signing was referred to as a *galáctico* by the media in an attempt to describe these players' aura and superstar status in the world game. The following year, in 2002, the club signed Ronaldo from Inter Milan for £26 million, David Beckham for £25 million in 2003, Michael Owen in 2004 and Robinho the year after that. Collectively they had become *Los Galácticos*.

Garrincha

[football] – *the legendary Brazilian player*

Manuel Francisco dos Santos was born on 28 October 1933 with a deformed spine, his right leg bent inwards and his left leg six centimetres shorter than the other. His sister Rosa pointed out that he was as small and defence-less as a little wren, a *garrincha*. Nevertheless, the diminutive Brazilian went on to win two World Cups and remains one of the greatest natural foot-ballers the game has ever seen. His ability to fly past defenders ensured the comparison to a little bird stuck, and the name remained with him for his whole life.

In one game in the 1958 World Cup against the USSR, having left a defender lunging desper-ately to the floor, he put his foot on the ball and offered his hand to help him up. Having hauled the Russian to his feet, he dribbled around him again and scampered off. Even in the biggest games of his career he would nutmeg* a player, run around him, wait for his victim to catch up and then nutmeg him again for good measure. He was brilliant, and the fact remains that Brazil never lost a single game when both he and Pelé were on the pitch.

During my time at the BBC I once flew out to Brazil to film a pre-World Cup piece about the history and brilliance of the country's national side. During filming, the great Garrincha agreed to take a series of free kicks against me. It wasn't a great idea on reflection, as one shot after another flew past the flailing BBC presenter!

* For more on *nutmeg* see Appendix, page 189.

getting spoons

[rowing] – *a crew being hit or overtaken in four consecutive races in the Oxford and Cambridge University Bumps*

The *wooden spoon* – given as a notional award for coming last in an event – originated at Cambridge University in the early 19th century. The Mathematics student that got the lowest mark in their exam but still earned a third-class degree used to receive an actual wooden spoon as a booby prize for their dubious achievement. This custom lasted until 1909 when the system was changed so that the exam results were given in alphabetical rather than score order, making it impossible to tell who had come last. Nevertheless, the concept of the wooden spoon was established.

In the Bumps races, a number of boats chase each other in single file, with each boat trying to hit the boat in front without being bumped from behind. If a boat manages to hit the boat in front it will be promoted to that starting position in the race the following day. By the end of the week, the ultimate aim of a crew is to progress to the front starting position, or *Head of the River*. This is traditionally celebrated by the crew and its boat club by the burning of one its old boats. It also entitles the winning crew to commission trophy oars in their college colours with the names and weights of the successful crew on them. These are known as the *winning blades*. However, if a crew is bumped on every single day and as a result find themselves at the back of the pack at the end of the week, then they are awarded a wooden spoon, or are said to be *getting spoons*.

God

[football] – *a nickname for the great Dennis Bergkamp*

According to legend, the *Flying Dutchman* is a ghost ship that can never go home, but is doomed to sail the seven seas for all eternity. Nevertheless, its name has leant itself to a number of Dutch footballers over the years, including my friend Dennis Bergkamp. However, after an incident at the World Cup in 1994 when a journalist sharing a flight with the Dutch side said he had a bomb in his bag and Dennis decided that he didn't want to fly anywhere anymore, the name became somewhat obsolete. Journalists instead toyed with the *Non-Flying Dutchman* for a while before moving onto the *Iceman* and the *Dutch Master*. However, it's no coincidence that his time at Arsenal has coincided with his major strike partners breaking the club's scoring record, not once, but twice, and so, based on his ability to see things no-one else can, many Arsenal fans have ended up simply calling him God.

Of all the great footballers that have played for Arsenal, I would place Dennis at the top. Until his arrival players were coached to pass a ball with only a certain degree of pace and weight. Nevertheless, he gave everyone at the club something to aspire to, having raised the bar of a player's ability to control a football to a whole new level.

golden sombrero

[baseball] – *the dubious feat of striking out four times in a single game*

This derives from the term *hat-trick**, which in the game of baseball was once reserved for a player who hit a single, double, triple and home run in the same game. Over time, however, it took on a far less positive meaning as it became a way of describing the ignominious achievement of striking out three times in a game. Since four is a larger number than three, the rationale of Don Baylor, the MLB stalwart who coined the phrase in 1989, was that it should be represented by a bigger hat, in this case a sombrero, which from above also looks like an awfully big zero.

A *platinum sombrero* or the *Olympic Rings* applies to a player striking out five times in a game, while a *titanium sombrero* is reserved for those who go one better and strike out six times in a single game. A titanium sombrero is also known as a *horn*, after Sam Horn, who accomplished the record feat while playing for the Baltimore Orioles in 1991.

* For more on *hat-trick* see Appendix, page 184.

goose-step

[rugby union] – *a hitch-kick motion performed while running that makes the practitioner appear as if he is slowing down when actually he is speeding up*

The goose-step, still seen on different military parade grounds across the world and most commonly associated today with the German armed forces of the Wehrmacht, was invented by a British Army officer as a way of testing if any of his soldiers were drunk. Nevertheless, it lends its name to a move that became synonymous with the highest international try-scorer of all time, Australian David Campese, in the late 1980s. The former Australian coach Bob Dwyer wrote in his book, *The Winning Way*, of Campese's move: 'An Argentine defender had Campese well covered, but when he moved to tackle him, Campese did his famous goose-step. The change of pace deceived the Argentinean so comprehensively that he dived into touch, clutching thin air. The referee, the Welshman Clive Norling, was so impressed by this that he went up to Campese as soon as he had scored and told him it was the best try he had ever seen.'

Green Hell

[motor racing] – *a nickname given to the infamous 24-kilometre section of the Nürburgring by three-time Formula One World Champion, Sir Jackie Stewart*

The 'old' Nürburgring is one of F1's ghosts – a 176-corner nightmare winding itself around the medieval castle of Nürburg and the surrounding Eifel Mountains. F1 drivers used to disappear for over seven minutes into the fifteen miles of trees and hedgerows that made up the *Green Hell*. 'I was always relieved when it was time to leave', Jackie Stewart explained. 'The only time you felt good thinking about the Ring was when you were a long way away, curled up at home in front of a warm fire on a long winter night. You know, I never did one more quick lap there than I absolutely had to.'

Niki Lauda's fiery crash in 1976, when he had to be pulled from the cockpit* of his burning car by four of his fellow competitors who stopped to help, confirmed what everyone had known for years – the track was simply too long to marshall properly. Although it spelled the end for F1 through the Green Hell, it's still regarded by many as the greatest racetrack ever built and remains open today for any members of the paying public crazy enough to take it on.

* For more on *cockpit* see Appendix, page 181.

Group of Death

[football] – *typically the most unpredictable group of a tournament because of every team in it being roughly the same standard*

The term was coined in Spanish as *el grupo de la muerte* by Uruguay coach Omar Borrás at the 1986 World Cup in Mexico. He was anxiously describing Group E, which included Denmark, Scotland, Uruguay and West Germany. There was no real cause for concern, however, as the format of the group stage at that time meant that only one team was eliminated. Somewhat inevitably, some might say, Scotland caught the first plane home.

gymnastics

[gymnastics] – *an artistic sport performed on various pieces of apparatus*

In ancient Greece, male athletes trained and competed in the nude. The name *gymnastics* comes from the ancient Greek *gymnos* meaning naked, or *gymnazein*, which means to exercise in the nude. As a result, women were excluded from the ancient Games, both as competitors and spectators. Shame!

hairpin

[motor racing] – *a 180° corner*

The hairpin corner is so called because from overhead it resembles the traditional thin double-pronged bobby pin used to fasten the hair. Probably the most famous hairpin in the world is *Rascasse*, the penultimate corner at the legendary Circuit de Monaco. Seven-time Formula 1 World Champion and five-time Monaco Grand Prix* winner, Michael Schumacher, did nothing to diminish the corner's fame in his last ever appearance at the circuit in 2006, when he used it to perform one of the most suspicious manoeuvres in the history of F1. Provisionally on pole* and with the qualifying session drawing to a close, Schumacher 'parked' his Ferrari at Rascasse, blocking the track and ensuring no-one behind him could improve upon their time. In spite of his claims that it was a genuine mistake, the FIA didn't see it that way and sent him to the back of the grid where he joined his team-mate, Felipe Massa, making it the first time in the history of the sport that the two Ferraris would start the race on the back row.

* For more on *Grand Prix* and *pole position* see Appendix, pages 182 and 192.

Hammers

[football] – *a nickname for West Ham United FC*

In 1895, the foreman of the shipbuilding department of Thames Ironworks suggested to the Managing Director, Arnold Hills, the possibility of the company forming its own football club. Hills – keen to improve morale in his workforce in the wake of a bitter industrial dispute with his employees – thought it was a good idea and established Thames Ironworks FC. By 1898, they had turned professional and been elected to the Southern League.

In 1900, having acquired another engineering firm, Hills and the board decided to make Thames

Ironworks a public company. Consequently, with shareholders to consider, they could no longer carry on pumping the company's money into the football club. Thames Ironworks FC was subsequently disbanded but, in its place, West Ham United Football Club Company Limited was formed.

By that stage Thames Ironworks FC has become known simply as the *Irons*, a name that carried over to the formation of West Ham and the name by which fans still refer to their club today. Over time, journalists created the name *Hammers* as another reference to their Ironworks origins, not as an extension of the word *Ham*, as is sometimes thought.

Hands of Stone

[boxing] – *a nickname for Panamanian Roberto Durán*

Roberto Durán is one of the greatest lightweight boxers of all time. Although only 5'7", he had a frighteningly strong punch that saw him win his first world title aged just 21. Legend has it that even as a fourteen-year-old boy his punch was so hard that when a friend dared him to hit a horse, he knocked it unconscious. By the time he finally retired in January 2002, aged 50, his punch had gained him the nickname *Manos de Piedra*, or *Hands of Stone*.

hare

[athletics] – *a pacemaker*

Like the hare at a greyhound track, the principal role of a pacemaker is to act as something to chase. A good pacemaker will be employed to establish a fast speed and rhythm for the prevailing pack early in the race before naturally dropping back because they set a pace they can't sustain. In theory this allows the stars of the show to go on and win. Nevertheless, it hasn't always worked out like that.

At the beginning of the 1980s the British ruled middle-distance running. Sebastian Coe and Steve Ovett lorded over the 1,500 metres and spent much of the summer of 1981 avoiding each other on the track. Later in the year, with Coe absent in a race in Oslo, Ovett (who'd set a world record in the same event on the same track the year before) figured he'd win easily, despite squaring off against a field that included Steve Cram and John Walker.

On the first lap, pacemaker American Tom Byers surged out in front and by the start of the second was ten metres ahead of the prevailing pack. Ovett and company decided he was going too fast and – knowing he couldn't keep it up for long – let him go. By the end of the second lap he was 40 metres ahead. The others assumed he had lost his mind and by the start of the final lap had allowed him to open up a 70-metre gap. The chase began. By the home straight Ovett had cut the American's lead in half and despite the Englishman ripping through his last lap in 52.3 seconds, it still saw him cross the line half a second behind the exhausted hare.

'I don't think they'd let it happen again', said Byers.

hare and hounds

[cross-country running] – *a type of race*

Although man has run since the beginning of time, cross-country running did not evolve as a sport until the 17th century. It came about in England as a result of the wealthy aristocracy wagering bets on the outcome of their servants racing on foot across their vast areas of land.

By the 19th century, it had become much more widespread as a sport, especially in English public schools where they had developed *hare and hounds*, or *paper chases*. In these races, an individual, or *hare*, would set off, throwing little pieces of paper as he went, providing a trail or *scent* for his fellow pupils, or *hounds*, to follow. This concept is still practised by running clubs across the world today, although many now use flour instead of paper. However, this caused alarm during the anthrax scares in 2001, and so the hares in many city-based running clubs now mark the pavement or road with a piece of coloured chalk instead.

Hell of the North

[cycling] – *a nickname for the famous 260-kilometre Paris–Roubaix one-day road race*

Started in 1896, the race is held annually in the mid-April rainy season, over the cobble-stoned roads and hard rutted tracks of northern France's coal-mining region. It has seen a number of horrific injuries over the years, but although fiercely difficult, this isn't how it acquired its nickname.

Immediately following the Great War, the course closely followed the largely abandoned front lines of battle and a consequent trail of devastation. Competitors cycled through mile after mile of ghostly ruins, trenches and rain-filled bomb craters and so to them, it was the *Hell of the North.*

Although the surroundings have been regenerated since then, the level of difficulty the course still poses means it has retained its name. Nevertheless, one man in particular has tamed it in its long and colourful history. Coming from a family of travelling clothiers, Belgian Roger De Vlaeminck, otherwise known as the *Gypsy*, entered the race fourteen times between 1969 and 1984 and never finished worse than seventh. He won the gruelling event a record four times, finished second four times and finished third once. All-in-all, a sufficient record to see him acquire the new moniker, *Monsieur Paris-Roubaix.*

Ike's Pond

[golf] – *a three-acre pond on the nine-hole course at the Augusta National Golf Club*

During his second visit to the Augusta National, General Dwight D. '*Ike*' Eisenhower went for a walk through the woods on the eastern part of the club grounds. On his return he informed the club's co-founder, Clifford Roberts, that he had found a perfect place to build a dam should the club ever want a fishpond. Soon after, the club did decide to build a pond and the architect heading up the project agreed exactly with Eisenhower's suggested location. Once built, it became known as *Ike's Pond*.

Imps

[football] – *a nickname for Lincoln City FC*

Formed in 1884, Lincoln City became a professional football club in 1891. The team takes its name from a twelve-inch tall gargoyle, high up in the east choir of Lincoln Cathedral. According to local legend, in the 14th century Satan sent two *imps* to Earth to conduct evil work. They first went to Chesterfield and twisted the church spire (see *Spireites*), before heading to Lincoln Cathedral. They started dancing on the altar, smashing up pews and tripping up the bishop, when suddenly an angel appeared. One of the imps cowered under a broken pew before making his escape. The other imp scampered to the top of a pillar and began to throw rocks at the angel. The irate angel turned the grinning imp to stone and it remains there to this day.

Indian dribble

[hockey] – *a dribbling technique whereby the player in possession of the ball pushes the ball rapidly from right to left and vice versa repeatedly while moving across the pitch*

In 1928, India entered a hockey team into the Olympic Games for the first time. They won the gold medal. In fact, they won the gold medal at the next five Olympics as well. During that era, India played 30 Olympic matches, winning all 30, scoring 178 goals and conceding only 7. They were, beyond any argument, the best team in the world. In 1956, they arrived at the Olympics with a new dribbling technique unlike anything the international hockey world had ever seen before. It helped ensure they won the gold medal without conceding a single goal. It was simply dubbed the *Indian dribble*, and is still the scourge of defenders to this day.

Invincibles

[football] – *the Arsenal side of 2003–04*

Between 7 May 2003 and 24 October 2004, Arsenal FC went 49 games unbeaten in the Premiership, amassing 121 points out of a possible 147. Although I know a few Spurs fans that will disagree, this record is unlikely to ever be surpassed. In the middle of that 596-day unbeaten run fell the whole 38-match season of 2003–04. They were *invincible* for an entire League campaign. But as I'm sure the same Spurs fans will be quick to point out, the term isn't exclusive to the mighty Arsenal. Several other teams have acquired the moniker over the years.

In 1982, the Australian national rugby league team toured Britain and France and won all 22 matches of their tour, running rampant and scoring 714 points while only conceding 100.

In 1948, a 40-year-old Don Bradman led the Australian cricket side on an unbeaten 32-match tour of England, which included a five-Test Ashes series which they won 4-0.

In 1924–25, the All Blacks toured England, Ireland, Scotland, Wales, France and Canada and returned home having won all 32 games and scored 838 points, while conceding only 116.

However, as far as Arsenal are concerned, I think it would be fair to say that they inherited the term from Preston North End, the only other team to have gone an entire season unbeaten in the top flight in the history of English football. Although their 1888–89 unbeaten season was sixteen games shorter than Arsenal's, that year Preston also became the first team to secure the Double, lifting the FA Cup without conceding a single goal! For that reason alone, they deserve their place in sporting history as the first ever team to be dubbed the *Invincibles*.

Iron Horse

[baseball] – *the nickname for Yankees legend, Lou Gehrig*

Until an aggressive form of motor neurone disease suddenly brought his career to an abrupt end in 1938, Lou Gehrig hadn't missed a single game in over fourteen years. He had played in 2,130 consecutive games, irrespective of any injuries he was nursing. Towards the end of the record-setting run, his hands were x-rayed, only to reveal seventeen different fractures that he had continued to play with throughout his career. His enduring reliability and consistency with the bat saw him nicknamed the *Iron Horse*.

In 1939, the Yankees retired Gehrig's number 4, making him the first sportsman in history to be afforded that honour.

Lions

[football] – *the nickname for Millwall FC*

Millwall Rovers was founded in 1885 by workers at Morton's jam factory on the Isle of Dogs. Although thrashed 5-0 in their first game, the side went unbeaten in their next twelve games and soon established a band of support. The club's location on the Isle of Dogs inevitably meant that a large proportion of their supporters worked in the area's docklands. Over the coming years this saw the team become known as the *Dockers*.

However, in 1900, the team reached the semi-final of the FA Cup and a newspaper journalist – so impressed with their acts of giant-killing while getting there – referred to them as the *Lions*. The club liked it and adopted it as their name, as well as a lion emblem bearing the legend *We Fear No Foe*. In 1910, the club then moved to a new stadium that they named the *Den*.

Long John

[golf] – *a nickname for John Daly*

Daly joined the PGA Tour in 1991 and as a rookie was the ninth and final reserve for a starting place in the USPGA later in the year. However, a series of late withdrawals saw the big man have to make a last-minute dash from his home in Arkansas to the Crooked Stick course, Indiana, where he shot a first-round 69 without even having time for a practice round. Daly's ability to hit the ball phenomenal distances off the tee with his driver played a huge part in his taming of the 7,200-yard course. He went on to shoot a 67, 69 and 71, winning him the tournament by three strokes. *Long John* had pulled off perhaps the most amazing win in the history of Major Championship golf.

Long Room

[cricket] – *the famous room at Lord's Cricket Ground*, which every player must go through before entering the field of play*

When English architect Thomas Verity built the Lord's Pavilion in 1889–90, he had already designed the Criterion Theatre, the Comedy Theatre, and assisted in the design of the Royal Albert Hall. He knew how to design a building as a viewing area and the Lord's pavilion was no exception.

As a result, he designed the *Long Room*, in which three walls are now adorned with the portraits of people like Lord Harris, Douglas Jardine and W.G. Grace, and the length of one wall is made up almost entirely of windows with a view directly out onto the square. It's at this window that MCC members

* For more on *Lord's* see Appendix, page 187.

have sat on their high stools for well over a century, dishing out advice to batsman as they pass through the room on their way out to face the music.

My only experience of the Long Room came in a charity debating event. Although an intimidating venue there's no question that it's an inspiring one as well, and I wittered on passionately about my goalkeeping hero, Manchester City's German prisoner-of-war Bert Trautmann.

As its name suggests, it's a big room, the sort of place you shouldn't miss when making your way around the Lord's Pavilion. That didn't stop David Steele holding up proceedings in the 1975 Lord's Ashes Test however, when, descending from the dressing room to go out to bat on his England debut, he missed it entirely and found himself in the basement toilets.

Lord Byron

[golf] – *a nickname for the great Byron Nelson*

In 1945, Texan Byron Nelson won eighteen PGA tournaments. This included a streak of eleven consecutive wins – a record that remains to this day and one very unlikely to ever be beaten. He also finished second seven times, was never out of the top ten and at one point played nineteen consecutive rounds under 70. His scoring average of 68.33 for a single season remained a record for 55 years, he hit a record score of 62 for eighteen holes and a record of 259 for 72. 1945 is still regarded as the greatest single year by a player on the PGA Tour. The following year, he retired, aged only 34.

Nelson's swing was so consistent and perfect that 30 years later it was used as a model for a robotic machine to test clubs and balls for the USGA. Another 30 years on, it is still in use and named *Iron Byron* in his honour. Nelson also conducted his career with such gentlemanly conduct that the renowned Atlanta-based sports-writer O.B. Keeler nicknamed him *Lord Byron* after the famous English poet. Ken Venturi, a former pupil of Nelson's and one-time US Open winner also said: 'You can always argue who was the greatest player, but Byron Nelson is the finest gentleman the game has ever known.'

Lucien Petit-Breton

[cycling] – *a pseudonym for Argentine cyclist Lucien Georges Mazan*

Born in Northern France in 1882, Lucien Mazan moved to Argentina with his parents when he was six. As a young man he won a bicycle in a lottery and never looked back – he was determined to race for a living. However, his father disapproved and was equally determined that he would do a 'real job' instead. This was very much like my own dad who refused to let me become a professional footballer until I had acquired a 'proper job' first. The young Mazan was forced to compete under the pseudonym of Lucien Breton so as to keep his occupation secret from his family. As if that wasn't annoying enough, he found out that there was already another professional cyclist with this name and so was forced to race as *Lucien Petit-Breton* instead. He went on to break the World Hour record with a distance of 41.11 kilometres. He also won the first edition of the Milan–San Remo, the Paris–Brussels, and the Tour de France in both 1907 and 1908, becoming the first person to do so twice. It was quite difficult to revert back to his original name after all that and so his pseudonym stuck until his death in 1917, during the First World War.

Magical Magyars

[football] – *a nickname for the legendary Hungarian National side of the 1950s*

For some years the Hungarian, or *Magyar* side was kept under wraps behind the Iron Curtain, but the beginning of the 1950s saw it unleashed upon an unsuspecting world. Between 14 May 1950 and 4 July 1954, the side went unbeaten for 32 international games – a record that stands to this day. The *Golden Team*, as they were otherwise known, was essentially built around six *magical* players. Gyula 'Black Panther' Grosics in goal, József 'Cucu' Bozsik at halfback, Zoltán Czibor on the left wing and forwards Sándor 'Golden Head' Kocsis, Nándor Hidegkuti and the legendary Ferenc 'Galloping Major' Puskás. During their unbeaten run, they became Olympic Champions in 1952 and winners of the Central European International Cup in 1953. The same year, they thrashed England 6-3 at Wembley (making them the first foreign side to beat England on home soil). This victory had worldwide significance as it effectively ended England's 90-year-old mythical reign since the creation of Association Football in 1863 over all foreign sides outside the British Isles. They then thrashed them again 7-1 when they met them in Budapest a year later (which remains England's largest ever defeat). They swept everyone aside in the 1954 World Cup in Switzerland, including West Germany who they beat 8-3, but who they would then also eventually inexplicably lose to in the final, 3-2. Their 32-match run had come to an end but only as a result of a match that the Germans felt compelled to dub the *Miracle of Berne*.

The Hungarian Revolution in 1956 and the subsequent occupation by the Soviet Union ultimately led to the disintegration of the great national side, but not before the *Magical Magyars* had made a massive impression on me as a youngster. So much so in fact, that they still remain one of my favourite international teams.

Magnolia Lane

[golf] – *the driveway from the front gates to the clubhouse of the Augusta National Golf Club*

In 1857, Belgian physician and amateur horticultur-alist Louis Berckmans established a nursery on a 365-acre site in Augusta, Georgia. One of the first things he did on the site was to plant a long row of magnolia trees from seed. In 1930, Bobby Jones bought the nursery from the Berckmans family for US$70,000 and although much of it made way for the golf course, the magnolia trees were kept and became the positioning for the club's drive. Sixty-one of the beautiful 150-year-old trees remain to this day, forging a tunnel along the 330-yard driveway that eventually spills out in front of the brilliant white Augusta National clubhouse. The American two-time Major winner Johnny Miller once described the awe-inspiring journey along *Magnolia Lane* as 'the quickest laxative in golf'.

Magpies

[football] – *a nickname for Newcastle United FC*

When Newcastle United began playing at St James's Park in 1892 they wore red shirts and over those, jerseys of red and white stripes. To avoid confusion with neighbouring Sunderland, they needed to change their strip. At a club board meeting on 2 August 1894: 'It was agreed that the Club's colours should be changed from red shirts and white knickers to black and white shirts (two-inch stripe) and dark knickers.' At no point in those official minutes does it state why they selected black and white. Here a few theories that have emerged over the years.

During the English Civil War, the Earl of Newcastle raised an army of volunteers on Tyneside to fight for the king. He assembled what would become the cream of the royalist infantry in the North. They wore black pants and hats, with black leather boots, belts and pouches and were known as the *Newcastle Whitecoats*, because of their coats of undyed wool. Over the following two years the Whitecoats, or *Newcastle's Lambs* as they were sometimes otherwise known, fought valiantly, securing much of the North. However, with the Scottish invasion of England in January 1644, Newcastle was faced with a war on two fronts and the Battle of Marston Moor six months later would prove too much. A combination of the Scottish Army in the North and a further three Parliamentarian armies attacking from the South saw Newcastle well and truly beaten. The Whitecoats ultimately fought to their deaths and it's perhaps for this heroic last stand that Newcastle's very own regiment and their signature black-and-white uniforms were honoured by Newcastle FC, exactly 250 years later.

Another theory is based on the close proximity of the city's Blackfriars monastery to St James's Park, and one of its 19th-century inhabitants, Dutchman Father Dalmatius Houtman. He was an ardent supporter of the team, spending much of his time at the ground. Some think that the club, inspired by the traditional black and white of his habit, adopted the colour scheme as their own.

Club folklore also talks of a pair of *magpies* that made their nest in the old Victorian Stand at St James's Park towards the end of the 19th century.

The team became so attached to them, and the supposed luck that a pair of magpies brings, that they insisted upon adopting the colours of the birds as their own.

However the decision was ultimately reached, this basic colour design of the home kit has remained resolutely unchanged since 1894, although the sock colour has occasionally changed from black to white over the years – notably during the Ruud Gullit era, who believed white was lucky. Either way, the black and white of their strip has seen them dubbed the *Magpies*.

Maiden

[golf] – *the legendary giant sand dune on the 172-yard, par-3 6th hole at Royal St Georges*

Towering to the left above the green, the giant hill takes its name from the fact that as you walk down the 5th fairway, the dunes between the 5th and 6th holes look like a *Maiden* lying down.

Over a century ago, the tee was positioned so that in order to hit the green, you had to 'fly the Maiden' and go straight over her, the ball often becoming hopelessly stuck in ruts or crashing into the sleepers on her face. However, in 1904, the tee was moved nearer the sea. Although further away from the green, Bernard Darwin, the great golf writer and St Georges club member wrote: 'There stands the Maiden; steep, sandy and terrible, with her face scarred and seamed with black timbers, but alas! we no longer have to drive her crown: we hardly do more than skirt the fringe of her garment.' Although she doesn't pose the problems she once did, she still looms as a potent reminder of many rounds she ruined in the past.

James Bond creator, Ian Fleming, was a keen member at Royal St Georges. Although shot at Stoke Park for the film, the golf scenes he set in the book *Goldfinger* were played at *Royal St Marks*, clearly a reference to his beloved course. This was confirmed by a reference by Bond to a giant sand dune called the *Virgin*.

married man's side

[darts] – *the left-hand side of a dartboard*

In 1936, prolific English novelist Rupert Croft-Cooke took time off from his fiction writing to compile a book about the game of darts – a pastime he loved. In it he wrote of the trouble for players trying for high scores and consequently always going for 20, but very often hitting the neighbouring 1 or 5 instead. If a player was to aim at the *married man's side*; the section on the left of the board that incorporated the 12, 9, 14, 11, 8 and 16, they wouldn't be likely to get less than 30 with their three darts, and so would probably post a reasonable although not outstanding score – the rationale being that a married man should always play safe.

Master Blaster

[cricket] – *a nickname for the great Sir Isaac Vivian Richards KBE*

'You knew he was coming', explains *Wisden's* Mike Selvey. 'The outgoing batsman would already have disappeared into the pavilion, and the expectation of what was to follow filled the air. Viv kept you waiting … time to ponder. Then he appeared, sauntering, swaggering, arms windmilling slowly. He would take guard, and then, head tilted back slightly and cudding his gum, he would walk a few paces down the pitch to tap it while looking the bowler in the eye. It was calculated menace and magnificent theatre from arguably the most devastating batsman of all time.'

'Occasionally, for no apparent reason, he would block an over in immaculate fashion, seemingly in defensive position before the ball had left the bowler's hand. Then, refreshed, off he would go again.'

Playing England at St John's in 1986, Richards confirmed his moniker when he took just 56 balls to hit the fastest Test century the game of cricket has ever seen.

Masters Club

[golf] – *a dinner held annually at the Augusta National Golf Club on the Tuesday of Masters* week for all previous winners of the tournament, hosted by the defending Champion*

In 1952, defending champion Ben Hogan gave a dinner for the ten other previous winners of the Masters. At the dinner he proposed the formation of the *Masters Club*, with its membership limited only to champions of the tournament plus the Golf Club's co-founders, Bobby Jones and Clifford Roberts. It was agreed that the Masters Club would get together each year for a similar dinner on the Tuesday before the tournament and as a certificate of membership, the defending champion would be presented with a gold locket in the shape of the Club emblem. The tradition has taken place every year since and although the Augusta National still

---

* For more on *Masters* see Appendix, page 188.

officially refer to it as the Masters Club, it has more commonly become known as the *Champions' Dinner*.

As well as hosting the dinner, the defending champion gets to choose the menu. Players have used this opportunity to show off the culinary delights of their home nation over the years, notably Canadian Mike Weir who chose Wild Boar, Arctic Char and Wapiti Elk, and Sandy Lyle, the wonderful haggis, neeps and tatties!

Mendoza line

[baseball] – *a batting average around .200*

This is considered the lowest limit of respectability for a professional hitter. The term is thought to take its name from the former successful shortstop Mario Mendoza. Although Mendoza finished with a career batting average of .215, the 1979 season saw him record an average of .198.

It's thought that the term then originated with Kansas City Royals star George Brett who, when asked about his own average soon after, responded: 'The first thing I look for in the Sunday papers is who is below the Mendoza line.' It should also be noted that Brett was full of praise for Mendoza's defensive qualities but as far as his assessment of his batting was concerned, the phrase stuck and is still very much in use today.

Mick the Miller

[greyhound racing] – *probably the most famous greyhound of all time*

He was born in Ireland in 1926, bred by a parish priest. The runt of a litter of twelve, he contracted a particularly virulent strain of canine distemper and almost died. As he slowly recovered, the priest named him after *Mick Miller*, an odd-job man who worked at the vicarage and tirelessly helped nurture the puppy back to health. In 1928, the priest took the jet-black greyhound to London's White City Stadium for his first ever race. He won, and never looked back. He went on to win a phenomenal 61 of his 81 starts, including the Derby in successive years, a feat not repeated for nearly half a century. He is perhaps the greatest racing greyhound that ever lived.

Monkeyhangers

[football] – *a nickname for Hartlepool United FC*

According to local legend, a large French ship was wrecked off the Hartlepool coast during the Napoleonic Wars. The only survivor was a monkey, who was washed ashore clinging to some wreckage and dressed in a French military uniform – presumably to amuse the ship's crew. The locals quickly held an impromptu trial on the beach. Being a monkey, it obviously didn't respond particularly well to their questioning and so, with its supposed refusal to give up any information, the locals came to the conclusion that it was a spy and should be sentenced to death. The unfortunate creature was promptly hanged, the mast of a fishing boat providing the makeshift gallows.

The Hartlepool United FC mascot is called *H'Angus the monkey*. In 2002, the man in the monkey costume stood for Hartlepool mayor 'for a laugh', dressed as H'Angus and offering free bananas for schoolchildren if he won. He did, and with his victory quickly found himself overseeing a £106 million budget and over 3,000 staff.

Murderer's Row

[baseball] – *a nickname given to the New York Yankees batting line-up of 1927*

Murderer's Row was a line of high-security prison cells at New York City's infamous 19th century Tombs prison. It housed condemned murderers and particularly violent criminals and lent its name to the World Series-winning Yankees batting order on account of them 'murdering' pretty much every pitcher that they met throughout their record-setting season of 1927, some of which remain to this day.

At that time games started at 3.30 pm and were often over by 6 o'clock, the Yankees line-up – which included the legendary Babe Ruth and Lou Gehrig – usually wrapping up proceedings in the late innings with the fatal blows that become known as *five o'clock lightning*.

musette

[cycling] – *a small cotton shoulder bag containing food that's handed to riders during a race*

Otherwise known by cyclists as the *bonk bag*, a *musette* takes its name from the French for a horse's nosebag. It's an essential item for a rider during a race because a lack of food will see their body run out of glycogen, the stored chemical the muscles burn for energy. In extreme cases, this can bring on a sudden state of delirium, known as the *bonk* or the *knock*, a marathon runner's equivalent of *hitting the wall*.

nassau

[golf] – *a type of informal game consisting of a given bet for the front nine, a given bet for the back nine and a final bet for the overall game*

This game takes its name from *Nassau* Country Club in Glen Cove, New York, where it was invented in 1900. At that time, inter-club matches were in vogue, and teams from Nassau CC, as well as those from other exclusive clubs in the New York area, had many high-profile members who were often in the news of the day. Although prominent members of the club, they weren't always great golfers and would sometimes lose their games by embarrassing margins. In order to avoid scores like 9 and 8, the club captain John B. Coles Tappan devised a system whereby, if you lost the entire match, the worst possible result could only be 3-0. With many of the high-profile members happier with the new concept, it caught on and as it spread to other clubs became known as the *nassau* way.

99 call

[rugby union] – *the infamous command of Willie John McBride MBE on the 1974 Lions* tour of South Africa*

When Irishman Willie John McBride led the British Lions to South Africa in 1974, no one had ever beaten the Springboks on home soil. Not even the All Blacks, and they had been trying for the best part of a century.

In the early games of their tour, the Lions were victims of a series of premeditated assaults by South African players, with home referees apparently turning a blind eye. In spite of this, the Lions won the first two Tests but when South Africa picked No. 8 Gerrie Sonnekus to play at scrum half for the third Test, it didn't take a genius to work out what they had in mind.

The late Gordon Brown, the Scotland second-row forward, recalled the lead of his captain: 'We had a meeting about how to react [to the violence]

---

* For more on *Lions* see Appendix, page 186.

and it fell to the big man to decide what to do. He took a long puff on his pipe, then he simply said, "From now on, boys, we get our retaliation in first". It was then that the "*99*" *call*, a cry to stamp out likely troublemakers, was born.'

It was decided that upon the hearing the words 'ninety-nine', each Lion would stop what they were doing and start fighting with the nearest South African to hand. 'There was method to the madness', McBride would later explain. 'You see, there were fights breaking out all over the place and some o' me lads were running 100 yards just to get a kick at a South African – retaliation like. Now that was no use to me. If someone like Gordon Brown, say, was fighting for 10 minutes that was 10 minutes he wasn't playing rugby. The "99 call" ensured everyone had a chance to settle their grievances and be ready to play 30 seconds later. Even a South African referee, so I reasoned, couldn't send off all 15 of us.'

McBride chose the 99 call as it was a shortening of 999 – the British telephone number for the emergency services.

Old Farm Derby

[football] – *a fixture between Ipswich Town and Norwich City FCs*

The two sides met for the first time on 15 November 1902. Local derbies* between the two clubs have become as important as one would expect from over a century's rivalry. Nevertheless, it's often referred to as the *Old Farm Derby*, a humorous reference to the *Old Firm* *Derby* between Celtic and Rangers, one of the oldest and most ferocious fixtures in world football. Similarly to Ipswich Town's recent acquisition of the nickname *Tractor Boys*, the reference to farming reflects the remote positioning of the two teams in the heart of agricultural Norfolk and Suffolk. They consequently play for the right to be called the *Pride of Anglia*.

* For more on *local derby* and *Old Firm* see Appendix, pages 186 and 190.

Old Mongoose

[boxing] – *a nickname for the legendary
Archie Moore*

Archie Moore made his professional debut during
the Great Depression of the 1930s, got his first
title shot with the advent of TV, and didn't hang
up his gloves until the outbreak of Beatlemania
three decades later. He's the only man to have
faced both Rocky Marciano and Muhammad Ali,
fighting the latter one month and one year before
his 50th birthday – an age that saw him nicknamed
Ancient Archie and the *Old Mongoose*. His career tally
of 145 knockouts is still a record and one that will
perhaps never be beaten.

perfume ball

[cricket] – *a bouncer on or just outside off-stump that passes within inches of the batsman's face*

Although the short-pitched delivery has been part of the game since it began, other than the Bodyline Series* of 1932–33, the bouncer didn't really become such a central part of a side's weaponry again until the great West Indian sides of the late 1970s and early 1980s. The deadly pace quartet of Joel Garner, Michael Holding, Andy Roberts and Malcolm Marshall would constantly fire in the *perfume ball* – so close to the batsman's face that he could smell it.

* For more on *bodyline* see Appendix, page 180.

Pichichi

[football] – *the individual top scorer in La Liga at the end of the season*

Rafael Moreno Aranzadi, or *Pichichi*, as he was otherwise known, played for Athletic Bilbao during the 1910s and 1920s. He became a legend in Bilbao, scoring the first ever goal at the San Mamés Stadium (or *La Catedral* as the fans still call it today), before going onto win the Copa del Rey four times with the club. Tragically, in 1922, aged only 29 and in his prime, he died after contracting typhus.

In 1926 a bust was erected outside the stadium in his honour. Teams visiting the stadium for the first time still pay homage to Pichichi by leaving a bouquet of flowers at its base. In 1953, the Spanish sports newspaper *Marca* introduced the *Trofeo Pichichi* to be awarded to the top scorer at the end of each season. Over half a century later the trophy is still in use, and if you win it, you are simply known as Pichichi.

Posh

[football] – *the nickname for Peterborough United FC*

Although Peterborough United wasn't formed until 1934, the team's nickname was decided for them over a decade earlier. At the beginning of the 1920s the club's present-day London Road ground was home to a side called Fletton United. At the end of a very poor season in 1921, Fletton's player–manager Pat Tirrel set about rebuilding his side in an attempt to win the Northamptonshire League. He declared that he was looking for 'posh players for a posh new team'. Although the side would later disband, Peterborough United FC inherited the nickname on its formation in 1934, and it has remained with them ever since.

priest

[fishing] – *a small club with which game fish can be quickly and humanely dispatched after capture*

Traditionally a *priest* would pray for a dying man or woman on their deathbed to help ensure a safe passage to God. These implements take their name from the fact that similarly, although perhaps a little more harshly, they administer the 'last rites' to the fish.

There is often a *marrow spoon* on the other end of a priest. These take their name from the traditional slender table utensil with dished ends with which a diner could extract marrow from a bone during a meal. Once the priest has been used to kill the fish, the marrow spoon is then used to extract the contents from its stomach. By doing so, a fisherman can choose the most suitable fly to use to try and catch more fish in the same stretch of water.

professional's side

[golf] – *the high side of the hole*

It's common sense that a putt that breaks below the hole has no chance of going in, but that still doesn't seem to stop me hitting it there! However, professionals know better and although they still miss putts with a difficult break, you'll very rarely see it miss on the low side. Above the hole, they give themselves the best chance of the ball going in, and so us lowly amateurs talk in admiration of the *professional's side*.

puck

[ice hockey] – *a hard black disc made of vulcanised rubber*

Although hockey* had been played in Britain in various guises for hundreds of years, it wasn't until the 1820s that people began to play it on ice. The idea was soon exported to the British protectorate of Canada and gained considerable interest in the second half of the 19th century. The certainty of long cold winters in Canada soon saw ice hockey become their national game. In the early years, a rubber ball was used but proved unsatisfactory because of the extreme bounce it generated on the hard ice.

Around that time the Victoria Skating Rink was built in Montreal. It was one of the world's first indoor ice rinks. Before long however, its owner had become fed up with the number of windows being broken at his new venue by the

---

* For more on *hockey* see Appendix, page 184.

volatile rubber balls. By 3 March 1875 he couldn't take it any more. On the sight of another breakage he stormed onto the ice with a knife, picked up the ball and cut it in half. The *puck*, albeit in need of a little modification, was born.

Though no one knows exactly how the puck got its name, some believe that it was chosen after the character in William Shakespeare's *A Midsummer Night's Dream*. Like the mischievous and irrepressible spirit, the puck moves frenziedly around the ice. However, it's more likely that it came from the verb *to puck* used in hurling for pushing or striking the ball – which in turn comes from the Gaelic word *puc* meaning to poke, punch or deliver a blow. Either way, many people these days simply call it the *biscuit*.

right church, wrong pew

[darts] – *a term for hitting a double, but the wrong number*

In more recent times this phrase has perhaps been more commonly superseded by *right house, wrong bed*. But its origins lie in the days of a more God-fearing nation when references to religion were far more common.

Darts has always been inextricably linked with betting, right back to its very beginnings with the throwing of arrows by archers in the Middle Ages. The game has therefore seen a large number of wagers over the centuries that have risen beyond a competitor's means. With so much at stake, and especially when going for a double, which would suggest it was nearing the end of the game, it was common for a player to say a little prayer on the *oche**before each dart.

* For more on *oche* see Appendix, page 189.

Rocket

[snooker] – *a nickname for Ronnie O'Sullivan*

Like Jimmy *'Whirlwind'* White before him and Alex *'Hurricane'* Higgins before that, Ronnie *'Rocket'* O'Sullivan, or the *Essex Exocet* as he's otherwise known, isn't slow around a snooker table. In the World Championship on 21 April 1997, he compiled the fastest maximum 147 break ever recorded. It took him five minutes and twenty seconds. That's an average of one shot every nine seconds.

Roland Garros

[tennis] – *the French Open*

Roland Garros was arguably the world's first real fighter pilot. After several missions in the First World War, he decided that flying and shooting was too difficult and so attached a forward-firing machine gun to his plane. The weapon despatched bullets through the rotating propeller to which he attached steel deflector plates for those that hit.

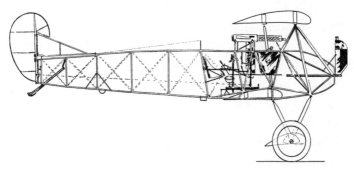

In March 1915, Garros shot down five German aircraft, an achievement that subsequently saw him dubbed an ace by an American newspaper. From that point on the term was attributed to any other Allied pilot that shot down five enemy planes while dogfighting.

The following month, however, he was shot down himself and forced to crash land behind German lines. He tried to burn his aircraft so as to protect the secret of his forward-firing machine gun, but was unsuccessful and was caught. He was placed in a German camp for the following three years until he escaped in February 1918 and promptly returned to service in France. On 5 October 1918, he was shot down again and killed near Vouziers, Ardennes, a month before the end of the war.

Nearly a decade later, in 1927, the celebrated French Davis Cup team, or Musketeers as they became known, pulled off one of the biggest shocks in 20th-century sport. They upset all the odds by winning the Cup on American soil, and in doing so, set up a rematch in 1928, in Paris. The occasion needed a stadium worthy of its stature and so the French Tennis Federation approached the Stade Français club for three hectares of land on which to build. Stade Français agreed, but only on the condition that the stadium be named after one of their most renowned former members – Monsieur Roland Garros. The venue has played host to the French Open ever since, and like Wimbledon, the tournament takes its official name from where it's played.

ruck

[rugby union] – *a phase of play where one or more players from each team, who are on their feet, in physical contact, close around the ball on the ground*

In Medieval Scandinavia, the word *ruke* was used to describe a *pile* or *heap*, usually of hay or fuel of some sort. The English adopted the word and over time it became *ruck*. It also acquired a selection of new meanings, its most common usage being to describe a large number or group of undistinguished people or things – very similar to a modern-day ruck in rugby in many ways. Although there are many rules governing the ruck, it sometimes just degenerates into a mass or throng of writhing bodies, not unlike the mass fights organised between rival villages in the Middle Ages.

Ruthian

[baseball] – *an adjective used to describe a particularly long hit*

Babe Ruth hit 714 home runs in his career, many travelling over 500 feet, earning him an assortment of nicknames, including the *Great Bambino*, the *Sultan of Swat* and the *Colossus of Clout*. On 18 July 1921 (the year that he hit at least one 500-foot home run in all eight American League cities), Ruth hit the ball out of Detroit's Navin Field stadium. It landed on the far side of the street, just under 600 feet away – verifiably the longest home run in the history of Major League Baseball. His consistent long-distance hitting saw the emergence of the adjective *Ruthian*, a term players still aspire to today.

The 46-ounce Louisville Slugger solid ash bat with which he hit the first ever home run at the new Yankee Stadium (or *The House that Ruth Built* as it quickly became known) on 18 April 1923, sold at Sotheby's in 2004 for a Ruthian US$1.26 million.

Scuderia

[motor racing] – *the Ferrari Formula One team*

Scuderia Ferrari is Italian for *Ferrari Stable*, which is often liberally translated as *Team Ferrari*. It's the name for the *Gestione Sportiva*, the division of the Ferrari automobile company concerned with racing. It was founded by Enzo Ferrari in 1929 as a sponsor for amateur drivers, racing mostly in Alfa Romeos until the production of the first true Ferrari car a decade later. The team then made its debut in Formula One a decade after that.

So although *Scuderia* literally means just *Stable*, it has become synonymous with Ferrari over the last half a century as the team has achieved unparalleled success in the sport.

The legions of passionate followers of the Scuderia are known as the *tifosi* – Italian for *fans*. A single fan is a *tifoso*, and a female fan is a *tifosa*.

Shot heard 'round the world

[miscellaneous] – *a phrase used to describe a number of dramatic moments in sports history*

In the final round of the 1935 Masters at Augusta, the legendary Gene Sarazen hit a 225-yard 4-wood on his second shot at the par-5 15th. It went in, and his *albatross* secured him a place in a play-off, which he won.

In 1951, the Brooklyn Dodgers and New York Giants finished level at the top of the National League and played a three-game play-off to decide the Championship. In the deciding game, trailing 4-2 with two men on base and a man out in the bottom of the ninth inning, Giants' Bobby

Thompson hit a home run, allowing himself and the two base runners to score, securing his team the title.

In 1976, in the Pheonix-Boston basketball championship series, Garfield Heard successfully fired an arcing turnaround jump shot over twenty feet to send the game into a third overtime.

In 1989, Paul Caligiuri curled a 35-yard strike over the Trinidad and Tobago goalkeeper and into the net, securing the USA a place in their first World Cup for 40 years.

The term often used to describe these moments originates from *Concord Hymn*, the classic poem written by American Ralph Waldo Emerson in 1837. In it he describes the impact of the battle of Old North Bridge on the first day of the American War of Independence:

> *By the rude bridge that arched the flood,*
> *Their flag to April's breeze unfurled;*
> *Here once the embattled farmers stood;*
> *And fired a shot heard 'round the world.*

skipping

[golf] – *the annual tradition during the practice rounds for the Masters whereby players try to reach the green at the 170-yard par-3 16th by hitting their ball along the surface of the pond from the tee*

Although it's cheating a little, the best approach – so I'm told – is to take your shot from the downslope of the bank just in front of the tee. That way, if you hit it at the right strength, the downslope creates the necessary spin to make the ball *skip* across the water. From that spot, and at that angle, five or six *skips* should see your ball onto the green. Any fewer and you haven't hit your ball hard enough and it will lose momentum and disappear into the pond.

It's worth knowing because if you skip the *skipping* as it were on a practice round in Masters week, you'll incite the wrath of the Augusta crowd. To avoid the boos, most try it in their own particular way. 'I toe in a long iron and try to hit a low hook that skips about six times', revealed three-time

Major winner Nick Price. 'That takes talent. Vijay can do it. He probably practices it – he practices everything else', he says with admiration.

Augusta's least official tradition began with the great Lee Trevino. He can't remember which year it was but he performed it in the tournament itself. 'I hadn't played well and was off early Sunday', recounted Trevino. 'It had rained a lot overnight, and the water on 16 was up to the bank. That water was perfect, like glass. I said, "Beautiful." I was about eight over par. That baby took three skips and ran up in the middle of the green, and I two-putted for par.'

slider

[cricket] – *a straight delivery by a wrist-spin bowler which is released from the front of the hand and deliberately floated to a full length. It then bounces less than the batsman might expect because of the backspin imparted on the ball*

It's a fairly common misconception that this delivery was invented by Shane Warne, when actually it has had several successful exponents over the years. The Australian leg-spinner Peter Philpott was using it in the 1960s, the great Richie Benaud before that and then another Australian, Doug Ring, before that. The confusion lies in the name.

After the Lord's Test in 1953, in which Benaud's bowling had been comfortably dealt with by Trevor Bailey and Willy Watson before Ring got them both out, the touring Australian side set off for Bristol by train. On the journey, Ring took an apple from the fruit bowl and used it to demonstrate the grip of his invention to Benaud, who before long would refer to it as his *sliding top-spinner*. Although much the same ball, Philpott would later call it an *orthodox backspinner*. It wasn't until Warne began to use it in such a destructive fashion three decades later that Richie Benaud, having become probably the best cricket sage and TV pundit in the world, would simply refer to it on air as the *slider*.

Slow Death

[cricket] – *a nickname for Jamaican umpire Steve Bucknor*

Stephen Anthony Bucknor is widely regarded as one the best umpires in the world. He has umpired more Test matches than anyone else in the history of the game. Nevertheless, it hasn't speeded up his decision-making while out in the middle over the years. 'I have never been hasty to make decisions', admits Bucknor. 'By nature, I like to take my time to do things. Patience is a virtue for me' – a comment that will resonate with thousands of batsmen the world over who have been made to wait in terror as he takes his lengthy trade-mark pause for thought while deciding whether or not to raise the finger of doom. If you see the characteristic nod, then you know you are about to be a victim of the *Slow Death*.

spaghetti-legs routine

[football] – *a goalkeeper's trick employed to distract a penalty taker*

Some goalkeepers pride themselves on their ability to out-psyche a penalty taker. However, they usually try and achieve it a little more subtly than Liverpool's Bruce Grobbelaar did at the penalty shoot-out of the European Cup Final vs. AS Roma in 1984.

Played in the Olympic Stadium in Rome, the partisan crowd went wild when Steve Nicol missed Liverpool's first penalty, but after Agostino Di Bartolomei and Phil Neal had made it 1-1, Bruno Conti missed to even things up. Graeme Souness, Ubaldo Righetti and Ian Rush were all successful before Francesco Graziani stepped up to take his. As Grobbelaar walked over to take his place in goal, his legs began to wobble dramatically in mock fear of the ensuing kick. Whether Grobbelaar's antics put Graziani off will never be known but the Italian sent his spot-kick sailing over the bar and Liverpool won their fourth European Cup.

Afterwards, Grobbelaar called it his *spaghetti-legs routine*. 'People said I was being disrespectful to their players, but I was just testing their concentration under pressure. I guess they failed that test.' In the Champions League Final 21 years later, another Italian side would fail the same test put to them by another Liverpool goalkeeper. Inspired by Grobbelaar's antics of the past, Jerzy Dudek replicated the routine and saved penalties from both Andrea Pirlo and Andriy Shevchenko to ensure the top European trophy returned to Anfield for the first time since 1984.

Having fought in a civil war in Zimbabwe, Grobbelaar could appreciate that football was not as important as some people would suggest. Nevertheless, he enjoyed thirteen successful seasons at Anfield, becoming the most decorated goalkeeper in league history. Then, in 1994, having moved onto Southampton, he was charged with match fixing during his time at Liverpool. I studied the games in question and had no hesitation in speaking on his behalf as an expert witness at three trials, which ended in his being found not guilty.

He believed that the match-fixing scandal arose because the press didn't like the person they perceived as arrogant and had a reputation for clowning around in games. 'Goalkeepers aren't supposed to do that', he reflected.

Spireites

[football] – *the nickname for Chesterfield FC*

The fourth oldest *football* club in England takes its name from the bizarre spire of the town's 14th century Parish Church of St Mary and All Saints. It rises to a height of 228 feet above the ground and leans perilously almost 10 feet to the south-west. What's more, from base to pinnacle it twists anticlockwise through more than 45°, and is still moving. The spire also just sits on top of the stone tower, balancing with no apparent fixing. How it remains standing I'm not quite sure.

Built in 1362, it remained straight for several centuries before it began to twist. There are several theories for the movements that have emerged over time. Some think that unseasoned or green timber was used; this was fairly common practice in the Middle Ages as it was less wearing on the tools of the time. Having said that, if green timber was used it was usually for less ambitious or permanent constructions than a 228-foot-high church spire! It's also thought that there may have been a shortage of skilled craftsmen at the time, after the Black Death had taken its toll on the area. Folklore also talks of two imps that were sent by Satan to do his evil work. Their first act was to twist the spire of Chesterfield Parish Church before heading off to wreak more havoc across the region (see *Imps*).

I have huge affection for the crooked spire. It was at this church in my hometown that I began a relationship with a girl called Margaret Miles which continues to this day, albeit as Mrs or Megs Wilson!

Springboks

[rugby union] – *the nickname for
the South African National Team*

In 1906, the South African national rugby union
team toured Britain for the first time. During the
tour, concerned that the British press were going to
coin an annoying nickname for their side, the team
manager, tour staff and team captain Paul Roos,
got together for an impromptu meeting in order
to come up with their own. Afterwards, Roos
informed journalists that they were to be called
De Springbokken. The *Daily Mail* duly obliged and
immediately ran an article referring to the team as
the *Springboks.* The team had a springbok badge
placed on the left breast pocket of their blazers and
the name has remained with them ever since.

Spurs

[football] – *a nickname for Tottenham Hotspur FC*

In 1882, boys from Haringey's Hotspur cricket club and the St John's Presbyterian local grammar school got together and decided to form a football club. Reputedly in a meeting under a street lamp on Tottenham High Street, close to the current ground, they decided to retain the cricket club name and simply call it Hotspur FC.

The cricketers among them had initially chosen the name Hotspur after the 14th century's Sir Henry Percy, or *Harry Hotspur* as he was otherwise known – the eldest son of the 1st Earl of Northumberland. By the 19th century, the Northumberland dynasty had significant ties with Haringey, owning large tracts of land in the area. Harry Hotspur was a great warrior and had acquired his new name as a result of the large riding spurs on his armour and fiery devil-may-care bravery in battle against the Scots towards the end of the 14th century. In 1403 he led a rebellion against Henry IV but was killed in the Battle of

Shrewsbury when hit in the mouth with an arrow. Something that your average Tottenham fan will forget to tell you at this point is that after his death Henry IV had his body quartered and sent to different corners of England and his head stuck on a pole at York's gates. However, his bravery and fiery temperament were later immortalised in William Shakepseare's Henry IV, Part I. Ironically, as a seventeen-year-old boy I played the part of Hotspur in our school play!

Throughout 1883, Hotspur FC were playing their matches on Tottenham marshes but it soon became apparent that they had to distinguish themselves from another team in the area going by the name of London Hotspur. So in 1884, they renamed themselves Tottenham Hotspur Football and Athletic Club, but before long, like the large, sharp spiked wheels on the heels of their hero's armour, they were simply known as the *Spurs*.

Sugar

[boxing] – *a nickname for – pound-for-pound – the best boxer of all time*

Walker Smith Jr. was born in Ailey, Georgia, on 3 May 1921. He began boxing soon after moving to New York, aged twelve. He tried to enter his first boxing tournament at fourteen but was turned away as he didn't have the necessary Amateur Athletic Union boxing card to prove he was sixteen. So he borrowed one from his friend, Ray Robinson, and went on to win the New York Golden Gloves Championship under that name. Upon seeing the young boxer fight for the first time, his future coach George Gainford exclaimed that his style was 'sweet as *sugar*'. Walter Smith Jr. had become *Sugar* Ray Robinson, and by the time he retired at the age of 44, he hadn't been knocked out once.

Texas wedge

[golf] – *a name for the putter when it's used to putt from off the green*

The term originated in the 1940s on the golf courses of Texas, USA, before being popularised by the great Ben Hogan. Without the high-tech irrigation systems that golf courses enjoy today, they used to rely on rain for their water. In the more arid parts of Texas this would often lead to very dry and hard fairways. As a result, players would often land their ball short in the hope that it would bounce up onto the green. This tactic would often see players drop it too short, with the ball coming to a stop before the green. In order to deal with the extremely hard fairway and very short grass, players would then often decide it best to pull out their *Texas wedge* so as to minimise the risk of their next shot.

Three Finger Brown

[baseball] – *a nickname for baseball legend, Mordecai Brown*

When feeding material into the corn-shredder on the farm aged seven, Mordecai Brown slipped and the machine removed much of his index finger while badly damaging the others. Doctors did their best to repair his hand but it was in a real mess. To make matters worse, while chasing a pig a few weeks later, he fell and broke several of the remaining finger bones in the same hand. Embarrassed by his second clumsy accident, he kept it quiet and so the bones were never reset. In time, they reformed, but in the most peculiar shape.

As Brown grew up, he worked in the Western Indiana coal mines, playing third base for the company baseball team at the weekends. Then in 1898, when Brown was 22, an injury to the team's pitcher forced Brown to the mound as an emergency replacement. It soon became apparent that the manner in which he had to grip the ball resulted in an abnormal amount of spin. He went onto become one of the best Major League Baseball pitchers of his era, and in the newspaper headlines, became *Three Finger Brown.*

tiger line

[golf] – *the most direct, and hence risky, line for a drive or approach shot*

The back or competition tee is often described as a *tiger tee*. Contrary to popular belief, this has nothing to do with Mr Woods. According to Peter Alliss, it comes from Sand Moor Golf Club in Leeds where model tigers were used to denote the back tees.

Similarly, the term *tiger line* has been in use since long before Woods was even born. In 1959, Ian Fleming described in his book *Goldfinger* the par-4 2nd hole at Royal St George's, Sandwich, as a 'three hundred and seventy yard dogleg to the left with deep cross-bunkers daring you to take the tiger's line' – meaning rather than go around the deep rough, go straight over it on the same line as a tiger would go through it.

This is why rough, bushes or trees on a golf course are also sometimes referred to as *jungle* or *tiger country*.

Timeless Test

[cricket] – *the final Test in the 1938–39 series between South Africa and England*

This match unsurprisingly brought the era of play-to-the-finish Tests to a close. It saw an aggregate of 1,981 runs scored over a period of ten days, 43 hours and sixteen minutes of playing time, yet still failed to produce a winner! After more than a week, England were finally set 696 to win in their second innings but on the tenth day, only 42 runs short and with five wickets still in hand, they were forced to abandon the game. It had gone on so long that they had to make a dash straight from the ground to their boat which had finally given up waiting and was about to set sail for England without them. The match was ruled a draw and would forever be known as the *Timeless Test*.

Tortoise

[athletics] – *the nickname for American Samoan,
Trevor Misapeka*

Trevor Misapeka went to the 2001 World Championships in Canada to compete in the shot put, but after a last-minute rule change left him ineligible, he decided to enter the 100 metre sprint instead, in spite of his 21-stone frame. His devastatingly slow 14.28 seconds brought him in over four seconds behind heat-winner Kim Collins. Nevertheless, the amiable Samoan was delighted: 'That's my personal best, I've never run that far before.'

He was affectionately nicknamed Trevor the *Tortoise* and went on to a more appropriate career as a defensive lineman in American Football.

Trotters

[football] – *a nickname for Bolton Wanderers FC*

In 1874, a team was formed at Christ Church Sunday school in Bolton. They played their games on the local recreation ground and used the school as their headquarters. They wore red-and-white quartered shirts and became known as the *Reds*. In time the vicar decided he didn't like the church's buildings being used as a meeting point for the football team without his presence and so put a stop to it.

On 28 August 1877, the team got together at the nearby Gladstone Hotel. Having now severed all ties with the Sunday school and consequently homeless, they agreed to call themselves the *Bolton Wanderers*. Although early in their wandering days, it was certainly a prophetic choice as they didn't settle at a permanent home for another eighteen years.

During that time, one of their pitches was next door to a working piggery. In reference to the name of pigs' feet and the frequent necessity for the players to *trot* through the slurry of the pigpens in order to retrieve the ball, they acquired the nickname, *Trotters*.

twelfth man

[football] – *a term often used to describe the fans of a team*

There is no doubting the effect of the twelfth man. The home World Cup victories of Uruguay (1930), Italy (1934), England (1966), Germany (1974), Argentina (1978) and France (1998) are no coincidence. A study by *The Times* in 2006 found that in the English Premiership, a home team can be expected to score 37.29 per cent more goals than an away team, this of course due in part to the benefit of the *twelfth man*.

The term originated in Dallas on 2 January 1922, when Texas A&M University were playing defending national champions, Centre College, in the American football Dixie Classic (the forerunner of today's Cotton Bowl). The ferocity of the game and resulting injuries ensured A&M ran out of reserves by the end of the first half. The only eleven remaining fit players were on the pitch. So the coach turned to the stands and from the A&M fans picked out E. King Gill as his possible back-up substitute. Gill agreed so swapped clothes with one of the injured players and stood ready on the touchline throughout the rest of the game. It turned out that there were no further injuries and so Gill was unused. Nevertheless, with his immediate willingness to help under the circumstances, ensured he had already written himself into A&M University folklore. He came to be known as the twelfth man.

After his graduation and subsequent departure from the university, all A&M students, in homage to that day in 1922, would remain standing for the duration of each game their team played as a gesture of their loyalty and readiness to play if asked. Over time, the team's loyal fans, and subsequently the University student body as a whole, also came to be known as the twelfth man.

Over the years, several sports clubs have retired the number 12 shirt so that they can dedicate it to their fans. These have included Bayern Munich, Torino, Boca Juniors, Feyenoord, and Portsmouth – 'Pompey Fans' being listed as player number 12 on the squad roster printed in each home programme.

Typhoon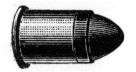

[cricket] – *a nickname for
the great Frank Tyson*

In terms of raw, unbridled pace, few bowlers in history come close. Richie Benaud and Don Bradman considered Tyson the quickest they ever saw. In a career plagued and ultimately curtailed by injury, he only played in seventeen Tests, but nevertheless took 76 wickets at an average and strike rate that put him in the ten most effective bowlers in history.

He acquired his nickname during his destruction of the Australian batting line-up on the 1954–55 Ashes tour. Having started off with 1 for 160 in defeat at Brisbane, he shortened his run and took ten wickets at Sydney and nine more at

Melbourne. The second innings saw him take 7 for 27 and some still regard it as one of the fastest spells of bowling in cricket history. The MCG curator was even caught illegally watering the pitch at night in an effort to stop it crumbling. The match saw Tyson confirmed *Typhoon*.

But it wasn't just his pace that earned him the name. He was a presence on the pitch, often quoting Shakespeare or Wordsworth to batsmen while out in the middle. In one match, during a hot frustrating afternoon for the England bowlers, Tyson managed to force an outside edge from the batsman that went right through the hands and then legs of Raman Subba Row at first slip. At the end of the over, Subba Row ran over to Tyson and said: 'Sorry, Frank. I should've closed my legs'. Tyson quipped: 'No, you bastard, your mother should have.'

War on the Shore

[golf] – *the 1991 Ryder Cup played at Kiawah Island in South Carolina, USA*

Like all Ryder Cups, the tension was unbearable, but this time, on the immaculate shores of Kiawah Island and the Atlantic Ocean, it was for all the wrong reasons. In the wake of the first Gulf War on the other side of the world, patriotism ran high, indicated by the terrible decision of Americans Cory Pavin and Steve Pate to play their golf in Desert Storm camouflage caps. The Europeans were not amused when a local radio station launched a 'wake up the enemy' campaign, making calls to their hotel rooms in the early hours. They weren't particularly impressed by the 'welcoming' dinner given in their honour either, which a US PGA official opened by solemnly praying to God for an American victory.

However, it was the action on the course that really started to see the accusations fly. Bernhard

Gallacher, the European captain, was convinced that Americans were listening in to his tactical team walkie-talkie transmissions. In the opening foursomes, Seve Ballesteros and José María Olazábal took on Paul Azinger and Chip Beck. On the 7th tee Ballesteros noticed Beck had changed the type of ball the Americans were using. 'I can tell you, we're not trying to cheat', Azinger claimed. 'Oh no. Breaking the rules and cheating are two different things', responded Ballesteros.

When Pate – injured in a car crash before the event – played happily on the second afternoon in his Desert Storm cap but was then withdrawn from the singles due to injury, some wondered if it had been done tactically. The failure of US captain Dave Stockton to tell his European counterpart of the withdrawal and the fact that it automatically secured the Americans a half point by default only served to fuel the accusations that followed.

It all amounted to what the less subtle sectors of the world's media decided to name *The War on the Shore*.

Wednesday

[football] – *an abbreviation of Sheffield Wednesday FC*

On the evening of Wednesday, 4 September 1867, the *Wednesday Cricket Club* met at the Adelphi public house in Sheffield. They took their name from the fact that Wednesday was traditionally the day that the local steel workers who formed the club took their half-day off to play sports. At the meeting, they decided to form a football team so as to keep the cricket side together and fit over the coming winter months. The rest, as they say, is history.

White Horse Final

[football] – *a name sometimes given to the 1923 FA Cup Final*

Wembley hosted its first final in 1923 having just been completed in under a year at a cost of £750,000. It saw Bolton take on West Ham in what turned out to be perhaps the most famous domestic final of all time. Although capacity for the new stadium was 127,000, the stadium entrances were not finished and so a far higher number of people made it into the ground. No one knows the final number but it's thought it could well have reached a quarter of a million with another 60,000 eventually locked outside.

With thousands having to spill onto the pitch, the game was about to be abandoned (despite the presence of King George V in the Royal Box) when mounted police were called in to push the crowds back to the sides of the playing surface. Among them was PC George Scorey and his famous thirteen-year-old white horse, Billie, who both actually had the day off but had reported for duty as word reached Scorey that the situation in the stadium had got out of hand.

Billie the horse was actually a grey but later appeared bright white in the high-contrast black-and-white newsreel footage and photography of the time. Although a number of other horses were also involved, Billie was the most distinguishable and so, much of the subsequent imagery gave the impression that he had controlled the vast throngs single-handedly. Billie consequently became a legend and the match became known as the White Horse Final.

During the match itself, the vast crowds had caused some fairly unusual moments for an FA Cup Final. When a player stepped up to take a corner or a throw-in, he had to wait while police negotiated him a run-up through the crowd that had formed a human wall around the perimeter of the entire pitch. Early in the first half Bolton's David Jack crashed in a shot hard enough to not only beat West Ham keeper Ted Hutton, but also

to knock a spectator unconscious who was pressed against the net behind the goal. Although the goal was good, it was made somewhat controversial by the fact that West Ham defender Jack Tresadern was still trapped in the crowd after taking the throw-in. In the second half, when Bolton scored their second to secure the Cup, the ball rebounded off the spectators behind the goal and back into play so quickly, that few people realised a goal had been scored. Never again would Wembley see such a vast crowd.

Wizard of the Dribble

[football] – *a nickname for the late great Stanley Matthews*

Sir Stanley Matthews is perhaps the best dribbler of a football the game has ever seen. He won the first ever European Footballer of the Year award, the first Football Writers' Association award, and was the first football player to be knighted for services to sport. His ability to evade a tackle with the ball at his feet was so acute that he was still playing in the top flight when he retired on 6 February 1965, just after his 50th birthday. Even at that age, he always maintained that he retired 'too early'. He was also the perfect gentleman – exemplified by the fact that despite playing in nearly 700 league games, he was never booked.

At 42, he remains the oldest player to have played in an England shirt. His England career is the longest of any player ever to play for the side, stretching from his debut on 29 September 1934 at the age of 19, to his last appearance on 15 May 1957, 23 years later. His international career saw him christened the *Magician* across the world.

Despite all this, arguably his greatest triumph came at Wembley on 2 May 1953 when he brought Blackpool back from 3-1 down with less than twenty minutes to play to beat the Bolton Wanderers 4-3 in the FA Cup Final. Despite his team-mate Stan Mortensen scoring a hat-trick in the game, his display of wizardry with the ball at his feet had such a profound effect on the game that it was subsequently dubbed the *Matthews Final.*

I was fortunate enough to meet Sir Stanley on more than one occasion and now treasure a copy of his autobiography in which he inscribed: 'To my pal Bob. With best wishes, Stan.'

WM

[football] – *a formation featuring five defenders and five attackers – three backs and two halves in defensive roles, and two inside forwards assisting the three attacking forwards*

In 1925 the offside rule was amended so that an attacking player needed only two opponents in front of him and not three as was the case before. This obviously made the offside trap much more difficult to execute and saw the number of goals in the English First Division rise 43 per cent from 1,192 to 1,703 the following year.

In response, the great Herbert Chapman and his Arsenal captain Charles Buchan devised a system whereby the centre-half was pulled back in to a centre-back role in order to deal with the now more dangerous and prolific centre forward. To fill up the gap created in midfield, the two inside forwards were pulled back to create a four-man midfield, or *magic square* as it would later become known. When all was said and done, the general shape of the defensive players made up a *W* and the attacking players, an *M* – a formation that became known as the *WM*.

Yo-Yos

[football] – *a nickname for Stirling Albion FC*

Stirling Albion had a reputation in the past of always being too good for one division but never quite good enough for the one above. In the 1950s they were promoted and relegated seven times, inspiring the saying in Scotland that somebody or something 'goes up and down like Stirling Albion'. The club's fans decided to make light of their predicament and so named their team the *Yo-yos*.

Zebras

[football] – *a nickname for Juventus FC*

Juventus FC was founded on 1 November 1897, by a group of boys aged between fourteen and seventeen. They played in pink shirts because it was the cheapest material available. Although the club grew quickly, entering the Italian Football Championship in 1900, they continued to use their pink shirts. However, as the number of games increased, so did the need to wash the shirts and they faded too quickly. So in 1903 the club decided to find a new kit. John Savage, an English player at the club at the time asked his friend to send over some shirts from England. His friend, being an ardent Notts County fan, sent a set of his beloved team's black-and-white striped shirts to Turin. Juventus have worn them ever since, becoming the *Zebras*.

Appendix

Definitions from Googlies, Nutmegs & Bogeys:

albatross

[golf] – *a score of three under par on a hole*

The term *albatross* came into use by golfers in the late 1930s in the UK and later across Europe, developing from the established **birdie** and **eagle**, which had been in use since earlier in the century. Most golfers never achieve an albatross in their entire career, as indicated by the rarity of bird chosen to represent this feat. Ab Smith, American co-creator of the term 'birdie' in 1899, referred to it as a *double eagle*, the name which most American golfers still use today.

birdie

[golf] – *a score of one under par on a hole*

In 19th-century American slang, the term 'bird' was used to describe anything good. Reputedly, *birdie* originated in golf in 1899, during a game between Ab Smith, his brother William Smith and George Crump at the Country Club in Atlantic City. On the *par*-4 second hole, Ab Smith hit his second shot to within inches of the hole and exclaimed he had hit 'a bird of a shot'. He suggested that if one of them played a hole in one under par, then that person should receive double the money from the others, and all agreed. He duly holed his putt to win with what they called, from that point on, a birdie.

bodyline

[cricket] – *fast bowling aimed at the batsman's body*

Also known as *fast leg theory*, this tactic was in use for some time before England's tour of 1932–33 when it was most infamously used, and named *bodyline* by the press. Douglas Jardine, the English captain on the tour, instructed his fast bowlers to bowl directly at the bodies of Australian batsmen in the hope of them directing easy catches to a stacked and close leg-side field. Although this tactic managed to keep the brilliant Don Bradman in check and consequently won England the Ashes, it caused several injuries to the Australian batsmen and became a full-blown political furore. 'I've not travelled 6,000 miles to make friends. I'm here to win the Ashes', was Jardine's response.

The laws of cricket came under scrutiny and saw several changes over the following decade to prevent another *Bodyline Series*, as it came to be known.

cockpit

[motor racing] – *the confined space in which the driver sits to control the car*

The first reference to this term dates back to 1587, when it was used to describe the pit dug to house cockfights. Over the following century, the term was applied to unpleasant places of combat on a more general level. Simultaneously – helped on its way by William Shakespeare, who in *Henry V* used the term to refer to the area around the stage with the lowest level of seating – it began to be used as a general term for sunken or confined spaces. For example, on British Naval vessels in the 17th and 18th centuries, the small, cramped area below deck – used as quarters for junior officers and for treating the wounded during battle – acquired the name, as did the area towards the stern of boats that houses the rudder controls. In this way, the meaning of *cockpit* developed to include any confined space used for control purposes. The term was taken up by pilots during the First World War, before finally being adopted by motor racing in the mid-1930s.

eagle

[golf] – *a score of two under par on a hole*

The term *eagle* began to be used by golfers in America in the 1920s as a development of the theme established by **birdie** earlier in the century. As the national symbol of the United States, the eagle was the obvious choice of bird, while it also represented the rarity and impressive nature of scoring two under **par** on a hole. It was adopted in Europe soon after and is now universally established across the golfing world.

furlong
[horse racing] – *a distance of one eighth of a mile*

For some time before the Norman Conquest in 1066, Saxon farmers in England had been using *furlongs* to measure distance. The word comes from the Old English *fuhrlang*, meaning *the length of a furrow*. It represented an eighth of a mile – theoretically, the ideal length for a field as it was the distance that a team of oxen could plough before needing a rest. Over time, this unit of distance was adopted by the horse-racing community.

Grand Prix
[motor racing] – *a type of race*

The first race to use this title was organised by the Automobile Club de France and run over two days at Le Mans in June 1906. It was won by the

Hungarian-born Ferencz Szisz, who covered the 700 miles in a Renault at an average speed of 63 mph. Although today the term is most commonly associated with Formula One, it was initially used to describe the principal race in a region, whatever class of car it may have been – the drivers were contesting the *Grand* or *Big Prize*. After the end of the First World War, interest in motor sport grew rapidly. A series of *Grand Prix* races across Europe were reserved exclusively for Formula One before an annual Grand Prix calendar was put in place.

Green Jacket

[golf] – *jacket worn by members of Augusta National Golf Club and awarded to winners of the Masters, which is played there*

This single-breasted jacket is coloured what is known as *Masters green*, and adorned with gold buttons and the club logo. It was introduced in 1937 and worn by club members during the **Masters** so that spectators could identify a reliable source of information. Although this practice continued, it was 1949 before what is now one of the most prized possessions in golf was awarded for the first time – the recipient was Sam Snead, the tournament champion for that year.

hat-trick

[cricket] – *the feat of taking three wickets with consecutive balls*

Although this term has now spread to other sports (notably football, for which it denotes that a player has scored three goals in a single match), its origin is in the game of cricket. In 1858 during a match at the Hyde Park ground in Sheffield, the bowler H.H. Stephenson – playing for an All-England XI – took three wickets with consecutive balls. It was customary at the time to reward outstanding sporting feats, so a collection was taken and used to buy a hat for Stephenson.

In time, this practice and expression made its way across the Atlantic to 1940s Toronto, where a haberdasher would award a free hat to any Maple Leaf ice-hockey player who scored three goals in a game. This in turn led to the tradition still seen today at North American ice-hockey games, whereby fans shower the ice with their hats when a player scores a *hat-trick*.

hockey

[hockey] – *a sport played with sticks, a ball and two goals by two teams of eleven players*

Although historical records indicate that *hockey* has been played in some form or other for over 4,000 years, it was not until the mid-1800s that it acquired its current name. At this time, a Colonel named John Hockey, while stationed at the garrison on Fort Edward, Nova Scotia, used a game very similar to the one we know today as a way of keeping his soldiers conditioned. These workouts soon came to be known as playing *Hockey's game*.

jockey

[horse racing] – *a person who rides horses in races as a profession*

The word *jockey* is thought to have surfaced around the end of the 15th century, as an extension of the Scottish name *Jock* which was, and still is, a generic Scottish term for a man or boy. In the following century, 'jockey' began to be used to describe men of an untrustworthy nature, and in time, the verb *to jockey* came to mean *to outsmart* or *to get the better of*. Although this propensity to trick or cheat didn't necessarily apply to racers of horses at the time, their job was principally to manoeuvre their horse into an advantageous position within a racing pack by any means necessary, and perhaps some early jockeys employed underhand tactics to do so.

Apprentice jockeys always have an asterisk after their name in an official race programme to denote them as such. Because of the symbol's supposed resemblance to a bug, apprentice jockeys are known as *bug boys*.

Lions

[rugby union] – *a touring side comprising players from the British Isles*

Lions rugby began in 1888, when sporting entrepreneurs Arthur Shrewsbury and Alfred Shaw, having already taken an English cricket side on a tour of Australia, decided to move on to rugby. Although they successfully took a team of British and Irish players to Australia in 1888, the first official tour – whereby a committee from all four Home Unions picked the squad – was for a South Africa tour in 1910, by which time they were called the British Isles Rugby Union Team. This name remained until the tour of 1924, again to South Africa. They set out with their somewhat cumbersome title intact, but returned as the Lions – the new moniker chosen by the players because of the lion standing proudly above the crest on their official ties.

local derby

[football] – *a fixture between rivals from the same district*

Although this term is most commonly used for football, it can be applied to any sport. It's thought to have originated with a tradition started in the Elizabethan era in the town of Ashbourne in *Derbyshire*, a few miles from where I was born in

Chesterfield. Each year, on Shrove Tuesday and Ash Wednesday, the people of the town board up shop windows and take to the streets to play the largest football match in the world. Although it is called the Ashbourne Royal Shrovetide Football Match, a fairly brutal game of rugby with fewer rules and a round ball might be a more accurate description. One team is made up of those born on the north side of the Henmore River, otherwise known as the Up'ards, and the other of those born on the south side – the Down'ards. The game kicks off at 2 pm and is then played until 10 pm on a pitch three miles long. As if that wasn't enough, much of it is played out in the cold waters of the Henmore, including the two goals, which were originally the wheels at the two local mills.

In my twelve years at Arsenal, there were rarely more important, competitive or violent encounters than our *local derbies* with Spurs, our North London rivals. Victory for one or the other was hugely important for both players and, of course, the fans, in what is always referred to as the *North London derby*.

Lord's

[cricket] – *the Test cricket ground and home of the Marylebone Cricket Club in St John's Wood, London*

In the first half of the 18th century, the nobility played their cricket in Islington's White Conduit

Fields, but as London's population grew, so did the players' impatience with the large crowds that appeared to watch. Looking to move elsewhere, they asked *Thomas Lord*, a bowler with White Conduit Cricket Club and an ambitious entrepreneur of the time, if he would be interested in setting up a new ground. Lord duly leased a ground on Dorset Fields in Marylebone, where he staged his first match on 31 May 1787 – and so the *Marylebone Cricket Club* (MCC) was born. A year later, the club produced a set of laws for the game, and to this day remains cricket's governing authority around the world.

MCC then moved to Marylebone Bank in Regent's Park for a short period between 1811 and 1814, before moving to a new rural ground in St John's Wood that previously had been the site of a simple country duck pond. This is still, however, the site on which *Lord's* cricket ground – the spiritual home of cricket – stands to this day.

Masters

[golf] – *tournament played every spring at the Augusta National Golf Club*

In 1934, Bobby Jones and Clifford Roberts, co-founders of the club, organised the inaugural Augusta National Invitation Tournament. Roberts had wanted to call it the *Masters* but Jones objected, thinking it too presumptuous. It kept its initial name for another five years, until Jones eventually relented and it officially became the Masters in 1939.

nutmeg

[football] – *a skilful move in which a player deliberately passes the ball through his opponent's legs and retrieves it on the other side*

A term that is thought to have been inspired by deceitful practice in the *nutmeg* trade during the Victorian era, whereby American exporters would cut their batches of nutmeg with similar looking bits of wood. The recipients deceived, or *nutmegged* as it came to be known, were left looking foolish, as is the victim of a nutmeg on a football field. In the current game, players affectionately use the term *nuts* when a team-mate or an opponent is on the receiving end of this skill.

oche

[darts] – *the line behind which a player has to stand when throwing darts*

This word was officially recognised by the British Darts Organisation only in the late 1970s. From the 1920s, the word *hockey* was used instead. Although the reason is unclear, it's thought that this came about because people used the crates from a West

Country brewery called *Hockey and Sons* to standardise the distance between the player and the board. The crates were two feet in length, so pubs used four of them to mark out the eight feet that was the standard distance for many years, and in some places, still is.

Over time, the *h* was dropped, so phonetically it became *ockey* and then acquired the new spelling, *oche*.

Old Firm
[football] – *Celtic and Rangers Football Clubs*

The rivalry between these two clubs is one of the oldest and most ferocious in world football, going back to when they first met at Celtic Park in 1888, watched by around 2,000 fans. Today, this collective term for these two Glaswegian clubs is used principally as a short nickname – for instance, when they meet in a **local derby**. However, when it was first used early in the 20th century, it was intended as a more scathing implication that the two clubs were in charge of Scottish football at that time, and ran it without consideration of other clubs. The term was chosen to signify the lucrative aspect of their frequent meetings, and the belief that the two clubs colluded to ensure their own profit and consequent domination, at the expense of the other Scottish clubs.

Whether this is true or not, no two teams across the world have dominated their national championship like Celtic and Rangers. As of 2007, between them they have won 92 of the 110 Scottish titles available since 1890.

Although I never knew him, a great uncle of mine – Sir John Ure Primrose – was Chairman of Rangers at the turn of the 20th century, and in 1902 he officially opened Hampden Park.

par

[golf] – *the benchmark score for quality play on a specific hole or course*

Some believe that *par* is an acronym of *professional average result* – although given the word's history this seems unlikely. It was originally used on the stock exchange, where a stock may be above or below its normal or par price. It was used in a golfing context for the first time in 1870, when golf writer A.H. Doleman asked James Anderson and David Strath, two competitors for the Open Championship at Prestwick, what score would win it. They thought that 49 would be sufficient on Prestwick's twelve holes, which Doleman subsequently labelled as par. The tournament was then won by Young Tom Morris with a score of two over par.

In time, different governing bodies across the golfing world standardised par to represent the score which all golfers should try to equal, if not better.

pole position

[motor racing] – *the number one slot on the starting grid*

Pole position is the optimal place to start a race from. Not only is it nearer the start line than any other car, it's also positioned so that the driver can take the first corner on the inside, and consequently shorter, line of the track. The term comes from horse-racing in the mid-19th century, when, if a horse 'had the pole', it had drawn the starting position nearest the post that denoted the starting line, on the inside boundary rails. It was adopted by the motor racing community in the 1950s.

steeplechase

[horse racing] – *a race of between two and four-and-a-half miles in length, over fences that are a minimum of four-and-a-half feet high*

In Ireland in 1752, 'a certain Mr Callaghan and his friend, Mr Edmund Blake, made a sporting wager to race cross country from Buttevant Church to the steeple of Saint Leger Church, a distance of roughly four-and-a-half miles'. This extract from a document found in the library of Dromoland Castle is believed to be an account of the birth of the *steeplechase* – a race in which orientation of the course was originally by churches and their steeples. This usually entailed negotiating whatever obstacles the countryside had to offer and, although this notion of diverse fences and ditches remains, the orientation by church does not. In spite of this, races such as the Grand National are still known as *steeplechases*.

Index